PLASTIC RADIOS

THE ANTIQUE RADIO COLLECTORS' SOURCE BOOK

CATALIN ▼ BAKELITE ▼ PLASKON
BEETLE ▼ TENITE ▼ STYRENE

BY MARK V. STEIN

RADIOMANIA BOOKS

Published by Radiomania® Books Copyright 2006

ISBN-13: 978-0-9647953-7-2
ISBN-10: 0-9647953-7-X
Printed in The United States of America

OTHER BOOKS BY MARK V. STEIN:

The Complete Price Guide to Antique Radios Series:

Tabletop Radios*, Volume 1

Tabletop Radios*, Volume 2

Tabletop Radios*, Volume 3

Tabletop Radios*, Volume 4

Pre-War Consoles

The Sears Silvertone Catalogs: 1930 - 1942

*Tabletop Radios series originally titled 'Machine Age to Jet Age'

The Collector's Guide to 20th Century Modern Clocks:

Volume 1 - Desk, Shelf and Decorative

Volume 2 - Wall and Mantle (in progress)

Further information regarding purchase of this and other titles directly
from Radiomania Books is available at the Radiomania.com web site
where all titles are offered at discount and all books purchased
are personally signed by the author.

WWW.RADIOMANIA.COM

Cover design by Jane Rubini
Book design by Mark V. Stein and Jane E. Rubini

ACKNOWLEDGEMENTS

This book was compiled from the archives of Radiomania® Books and would not have been possible without the contribution of resources, time and assistance from many enthusiasts. In particular we would like to thank the following:

Mark Alzapiedi, Martin Bergen, Al Bernard, Radio Bill from Detroit, Richard Bosch, George Breckenridge, Steve Caiati, Steve Chapman, Jim Clark, Allen Cutts, Mark Delauter, Ted Depto, Spencer Doggett, Larry Dowell, Bruce Eddy, Mike Emery, John England, Carlos, Lazarini Fonesca, Steve Fullmer, Ira Grossman, Joel Halser, Phil Harris, Doug Heimstead, W .F. Horn, Don Howland, Alan Jesperson, Johnny Johnson, George Kaczowka, Bob Kaminsky, Jay Kiessling, Richard Loban, Merrill Mabbs, Jay Malkin, Aaron Mall, Ben Martin, David Mednick, Jim Meehan, Fito Mirkin, Frank Moore, Rev. Maurice S. Moore, Phil Nelson, Bob Peklo, John Pelham, Robert Prince, Jennifer Purkis, Rod Rogers, Jerry Rose, Stan Rosenstein, John Sakas, Steven Sandler, Geoff Shearer, Thomas Seller, Mike Stambaugh, Jon Steinhauser, Larry Stencel, Sid Stivland, Ted's Vintage Radios, Marion Van Hill, Barney Van Horn, Alan Voorhees, Jim Watson and Barry Zimmerman.

BASIS FOR STATED VALUES

For purposes of this guide, listed values are for radios in fully intact and original condition. The cabinet is free from chips, breaks, cracks, deep scuffs and burns. Superficial discoloration from the passage of time is acceptable. Electronics are original and complete and the radio likely not to be in working order.

Because the same cabinet may have been marketed with several different chassis and under more than one brand name, an effort to list one representative model of each type has been made. In most cases we have chosen a standard 5-tube single band AC model. The stated value is for the model with the specifications indicated. Variations in bands, tube count and power source will impact the value. Please review "General Guidelines for Assessing Value" for further insight.

NOTICE: *The market values indicated in this reference are based on a number of sources. Actual prices will vary dependent on many variables. Neither the author nor the publisher assumes responsibility for losses which might result from the use of this book.*

TABLE OF CONTENTS

RATIONALE FOR LISTED VALUES

As most collectors are aware, even the best price guide, if not initially flawed, is soon obsolete. In the field of antique radios, pegging a value is made even more difficult by the number of variables which must be considered. Radios are less a "commodity" than other collectibles, such as coins, stamps and comic books, and do not easily lend themselves to grading. The tremendous number of manufacturers, brand names and models makes the basic task of cataloging a daunting one. Value for radios must consider the housing, chassis and other components. A simple grade of "excellent" means little without context.

Even with all attributes being the same, the range of prices paid for any given radio is wide and variable. Prices at garage sales, antique shops and auctions differ greatly. Valuable catalin radios continue to sell for five or ten dollars at garage sales, although certainly not as often as used to be the case. Antique shops increasingly price radios worth twenty dollars at two hundred. And we have all witnessed the effect of two eager bidders on the final price of a radio at auction. Thus, the task of establishing a reliable 'market value' is next to impossible. It is therefore suggested that the stated values be used more as a general market gauge.

The above disclaimer having been made, a sincere and methodical effort has been made to establish rational values for this guide. Multiple resources were accessed wherever possible. Because an increasingly large proportion of antique radios are changing hands at on-line auction sites such as eBay, Yahoo! and Amazon, we have made extensive efforts to cull prices from completed auctions. We have also identified new trends in values, which are now beginning on the internet. We also considered traditional auction results, classified ads, collector meets, and expert opinions, including the author's personal experience having been both a collector and dealer for over twenty years.

OVERVIEW OF PLASTICS

The value of plastics to technology, mass production and our lifestyles today can not be overstated. Countless new technologies, products and industries would not exist were it not for these unique compounds. Plastics have been synthesized to resist heat, insulate electricity, and to minimize breakage. They can be made rigid or elastic, opaque or transparent, colorless or kaleidoscopic. Their variation and uses continue to expand daily.

The history of plastics can be traced back to the early 19th century. Naturally occurring plastics such as rubber, waxes and even horn were molded into consumer products. They quickly became an integral part of the forming industrial revolution, a revolution of consumer goods, from piecemeal to mass production. The evolution of plastics also demonstrates the continued and constant quest by science and industry to improve and expand their utility.

HISTORIC DEVELOPMENT

The first "synthesized" plastic was made in 1839 when Charles Goodyear added sulfur to natural rubber, a naturally occurring plastic, to create "vulcanized" rubber. The addition of sulfur increased the life, durability and elasticity of rubber products. In 1847 gutta percha, natural latex, was introduced and by 1850 it was being used as an insulator for underwater telegraph cables. A decade later, Alexander Parkes created cellulose-nitrate. The British Parkes was looking for a synthetic substitute for ivory pool balls. He discovered that dissolving cellulose in a solution with nitric acid created a reaction which caused the liquid cellulose-nitrate to harden into a material resembling ivory. He introduced his "synthetic ivory" at the 1862 London Worlds' Fair under the brand name "Parkesine". Parkes' enterprise quickly failed, however, in 1863 John Wesley Hyatt successfully launched his own cellulose-nitrate enterprise naming his product "celluloid". Hyatt had both the vision for products and the wherewithal to design machinery for their manufacture. He produced everything from false teeth to collar stays. Later his celluloid was used in movie film. Hyatt also mass-produced and marketed decorative celluloid items for consumers, such as the combs and hand mirrors.

By the turn of the century, other types of cellulose based plastics were being used in production. Cellulose-acetate, also known as "Tenite", was developed as a non-flammable alternative to cellulose-nitrate and became the first plastic to be injection molded. Cellulose-acetate's durability was improved upon by adding butyric acid in the solution and creating cellulose acetate butyrate.

The next great evolutionary leap for plastics was in 1909 when Leo Hendrik Baekelund introduced "Bakelite", the first phenolic plastic. In his efforts to create a new type of insulating shellac, Baekelund discovered that heat applied to a mixture of phenol and formaldehyde created a syrupy liquid, now referred to as a phenolic resin, which became quite hard when cooled. He was able to increase the integrity of molded items by applying pressure to the hot resin to force out pockets of air. His process and product were patented and by the 1920's Bakelite was widely used in the production of both industrial and consumers goods. Bakelite was dark by nature and its palette was limited to black and various hues of brown.

In order to make products more appealing, a search for a light or colorless plastic which could be dyed or tinted with different colors was begun. This search resulted in the development of two new plastics: catalin and urea formaldehyde. German researchers developed a transparent type of phenol resin which they named "catalin". Special dyes were developed and employed to produce magnificent marbled effects. The second new plastic, urea-formaldehyde, was developed by researchers in the United States. They combined carbon-dioxide and ammonia with formaldehyde to create a pale white opaque plastic very similar to bakelite in most other ways. When dyes were added to the plastic resin, the resulting hardened plastic was brilliant in color. Some dying techniques produced speckled or marbled plastics. Trade names for urea-formaldehyde included "beetle" and "Plaskon".

By the late 1930's both polystyrene, "styrene", and polymethyl-methacrylate "acrylic" had been developed. Styrene is colorless and easily tinted. Acrylic is typically transparent or translucent in the final product. Both were initially cost-prohibitive to produce, however, the Second World War provided a strong incentive to use plastics as substitutes for depleted conventional resources. The resulting new chemical and production technologies for plastics expanded the industry exponentially by the end of the war. By the late 1950's polystyrene was the dominant plastic in use for consumer products due to its now low cost and ease of production using new injection mold technology.

PLASTIC IDENTIFICATION AND NAMING CONVENTIONS

For the novice collector the names of different plastics used in the manufacture of radio cabinets can be confusing. Furthermore, the names we use today have been established more from convention than science. That is, most all of the descriptive names currently used were at one time a brand or product name for the material. Typically, many manufacturers produced the same or a similar material. For one reason or another a single brand name has, over time, become synonymous with the material itself. The most common types of radio plastics and their conventions are as follows:

Bakelite was the first plastic used for radio cabinets beginning in the early 1930's. Bakelite was the primary trade name for phenol-formaldehyde. The plastic was made by heating a mixture of phenol and formaldehyde until it became a thick syrupy resin. As it cooled it became extremely hard. The molding process also used intense pressure to force out air bubbles which had formed during the reaction. Molded bakelite products could be highly detailed and complex. The surface of molded bakelite is porous, although waxes and polishes can be used to create a smooth shiny appearance. The chemical nature of bakelite limits its coloration to black, shades of brown and very dark red. Some molding processes produced a marbled effect of dark and light brown tones to varying degrees. Bakelite does not deteriorate with time. It is also an excellent insulator, making it well suited for use in housings for radios and other electronics.

Catalin was deliberate variation of the basic bakelite formula which resulted in clear phenol resin. The clear resin was was mixed with special color dyes, poured into casting molds and cured in low heat ovens over a period of days. Only very basic designs, with little detail could survive the molding extraction process. Many cabinets were still broken during removal from the mold. Those items surviving extraction were manually machined to remove debris and to add detail to the design. The intensity of labor required to produce catalin products was not an issue in the late 1930's when it was first introduced. After World War II the shortage of manpower and its accompanying ncreased cost made catalin use cost prohibitive.

Catalin is the most valued of plastics used in radios. It polishes to a mirror-like sheen. Coloration ranges from opaque solid colors to translucent swirls of color resembling polished agate. It is, however, prone to chips, cracks, burns (from tube heat), and discoloration. Catalin also shrinks slightly over time, eventually causing cracks when this shrinkage competes with a metal chassis. Such hazards impact the number of catalin sets which have survived fully intact and thus their price.

Plaskon, Beetle and Urea all refer to types of urea-formaldehyde, a resin similar to bakelite, molded using heat and intense pressure. Urea-formaldehyde products were marketed under a variety of brand names including "Plaskon" and "Beetle". The unadulterated plastic is an opaque pale white or cream color. Use of dyes resulted in striking colors in addition to speckled and marbled effects. Urea formaldehyde was used to mold cabinets from the mid-1930's through the 1950's. It is less porous than bakelite and more easily polished. It is also an excellent insulator and equally resistant to impact. Urea formaldehyde is, however, a less stable plastic. Surfaces may exhibit hairline cracks from the stress of the original molding process after the passage of time. Another unfavorable aspect of this plastic, particularly with white, is its susceptibility to discoloration from exposure to the ultraviolet rays of sunlight. An ivory radio left in the sun will be darker, sometimes approaching gray, after several hours of exposure. Any area on the surface which is protected from the sun will not change in color.

Although the same chemical substance, there are three different names used by collectors to refer to urea-formaldehyde dependent on color, pattern and vintage:

Plaskon typically refers to all solid colored urea formaldehyde radio cabinets. Pre-war cabinets were primarily white, however brilliant red, pistachio green, sky blue and canary yellow were occasionally available options and are now highly prized by collectors.

Urea is sometimes used to refer to urea-formaldehyde radio cabinets made after 1945. The color palette was different and more greatly varied, including both pastels and vivid colors. For purposes of this book, and for many collectors, the term "Plaskon" is used when referring both to pre- and post-war urea-formaldehyde solid color cabinets.

Beetle refers to pale white urea formaldehyde with marbling of various colors. Some examples of beetle may be subtle: pale white with just a hint of rust marbling, while others evidence themselves in a wide array of deep oranges, greens, blues, reds and browns.

Tenite, or cellulose-acetate, was developed as a non-flammable alternative to cellulose-nitrate, "celluloid". It was the first plastic to be injection molded. It was slightly more flexible than bakelite and well suited for small, high contact parts. A significant number of radio knobs, grills, handles and dial bezels were made from tenite during the 1930's and 1940's. Unfortunately, this material did deteriorate over time. Tenite's durability was later improved upon by adding butyric acid, creating cellulose-acetate-butyrate. Butyric acid is the culprit of the odor sour milk's odor. It is easy to tell if a vintage part is made from cellulose-acetate-butyrate. The smell is unforgettable.

Styrene or polystyrene is a colorless and easily tinted plastic. It is more brittle than bakelite and less porous. Styrene does not deteriorate over time like other plastics but is more prone to chipping and melts when exposed to heat. Due to its low cost and ease of production using new injection mold technology, ploystyrene has been the dominant plastic used for consumer products since the late 1950's.

SOURCES:

Carley, James. Whittington's Dictionary of Plastics, Third Edition. Lancaster: Technomic Publishing Company, 1993

DuBois, J. Harry. Plastics history U.S.A. Boston: Cahners, 1972.

Meikle, Jeffrey. American Plastic: A Cultural History. New Brunswick: Rutgers University Press, 1995.

Modern Plastics Encyclopedia. New York: Plastics Catalogue Corporation, 1946.

"Gutta Percha". Transatlantic Cable Communications. 2005.
http://collections.ic.gc.ca/cable/gutta.htm

"The History of Plastic". 2006. American Plastics Council.
<http://www.americanplasticscouncil.org/s_apc/sec.asp?CID=310&DID=920>

"The History of Plastics". 2003. British Plastics Federation.
<http://www.bpf.co.uk/bpfindustry/History_of_Plastics.cfm>

VALUING PLASTIC RADIOS

CHIPS AND CRACKS

As a rule of thumb, a major flaw in any plastic radio, such as a significant visible chip, crack or warp, will cut the value of that radio in half so long as it remains displayable. Among Plaskon radios, superficial stress cracks are fairly common. In many models they are the rule and not the exception. So long as the stress lines are not too numerous and do not detract materially from the general aesthetics of the radio, the depreciation should be minimal. On the other hand, the stress free example of a set which is commonly found with stress lines is worth considerably more than average.

FRAGILITY

Dependent on the thickness of the casting, materials used in construction and the extremity of design, some radios are inherently more delicate than others. The most fragile (such as the Kadette 'Classic') are rarely found in near perfect condition. This 'universe' from which each radio is drawn must be considered in determining its value. In our example, a Kadette 'Classic' in what would appear to the casual observer as marginal condition, might, in fact, be an excellent example of that model, given the condition of other surviving sets.

REPAIRS

Although there have been some relatively successful attempts at bakelite repair, no repair can go undetected. A well repaired flaw can increase the value of a radio but will never raise its value to that of an unflawed one.

PAINT CHIPS

Early bakelite radios were typically offered in a painted ivory finish. The painted cabinet was baked for several hours so as to make the finish more durable. This cured paint finish is susceptible to chipping over time. Cured paint finishes are much more difficult to remove even with caustic paint stripping chemicals. Once the a cabinet is stripped, you may discover the trim no longer matches the cabinet. As a rule of thumb, the value of a cured paint radio with chipped finish is reduced by anywhere from ten to fifty percent dependent on the extent and placement of chipping.

GENERAL CONSIDERATIONS

General rules of thumb apply when valuing a potential addition to your collection. Please remember, as with all rules, there are always exceptions. If you are at all uncertain about a radio, you will do best to ask a trusted collector or a knowledgeable appraiser.

INDUSTRIAL DESIGN

In the early part of the twentieth century the proliferation of mass production created a rift among craftsmen. William Morris and the "Arts and Crafts" movement saw mass production as the end of artistry in utilitarian goods. Walter Gropius and the Bauhaus viewed industrialization as inevitable. Their partnerships with industry infused a new "modern" artistic sensibility into manufactured goods. The impact from the financial success of the Bauhaus and related movements was worldwide. By the end of the 1920's a credible art form had emerged from the marriage of art and industry: "Industrial Design".

Much attention is now being paid by collectors and curators to manufactured items of artistic caliber. The recently coined term "Design Pedigree" refers to a manufactured item which is the documented creation of a noteworthy designer. Industrial designers including John Vassos, Gilbert Rohde, Henry Dreyfuss, Walter Dorwin Teague, Norman Bel Geddes and Russell Wright have all designed radio cabinets for major manufacturers. The documented association of a radio with a noteworthy designer will greatly worth.

BRAND NAME

Among collectors, certain brands are desirable in and of themselves. Often times, the rationale might be the city in which the manufacturer was located. Examples of such brands include Detrola (Detroit), Simplex (Sandusky, OH), and several Los Angeles manufacturers including Troy, Herbert Horn/Tiffany Tone, Gilfillan, Packard-Bell and Jackson-Bell.

Other rationales for collecting a specific brand include quality (e.g., Atwater Kent, Stromberg-Carlson, Zenith, EH Scott, McMurdo Silver) and design diversity (e.g., General Television, Climax, Clinton). Many collectors focusing on a single brand compete furiously for new acquisitions to round out their collection.

TUBE AND BAND COUNTS

Tube and band counts are both general indicators of a radio's position in the production line for a given year. Although single band radios were the rule until 1934, tube counts varied in these early years, generally with as few as four tubes and ranging to twelve or fifteen. The number of tubes determined the cost and complexity of the circuitry. More tubes indicated greater sensitivity, fidelity and power amplification. Beginning in 1934 two band radios (broadcast/shortwave) radios were introduced in mass production. In 1935 the shortwave bands were further divided into smaller band ranges. Tube counts were generally correlated with band counts from 1935 onward, with both increasing in number, the higher one went in a given manufacturer's product line. The higher the rank in the production line, the greater the cost to the consumer. This usually translated into lower production numbers. The number of high end radios surviving today is thus extremely limited.

POWER SOURCE

Most of rural America was not 'electrified' in the 1930's. Therefore, many radios were designed for operation with direct current power. The power source might be one, two or three batteries (A, B & C Batteries). DC power was also provided by motor generators and windmills (i.e., Zenith's Wincharger). Input voltage also varied widely. When evaluating the worth of a vintage radio, the power source, AC vs. DC, is important. A DC powered radio will require modification or a converter if it is to be operational. Conversion cost ranges around $50-100. Even with a converter, a DC powered radio is less desirable and therefore less valuable than an equivalent AC set. This value differential is typically 25-50%.

EVALUATING CHASSIS AND TRIM

In buying any vintage radio it is important to visually inspect the chassis, particularly if you plan to restore the set to working order. Additionally, the absence of, or damage to, trim pieces is important. Here are some general guidelines to keep when evaluating a chassis and trim.

CHASSIS CORROSION

Minor chassis surface oxidation/corrosion is typical and acceptable to all but the most finicky of collectors and should not deter from the value. Extreme corrosion can be an indication that the radio was submerged at one time or at least has seen a lot of humidity. If so, the bulk of the internal components may need to be replaced. Even if you plan only to display the radio, such damage decreases its value by virtue of the fact that it is less desirable to most other collectors.

RODENT DAMAGE

Most of us have, at some time, come across a radio the chassis of which has been stuffed with leaves, feathers, pieces of acorns and other unlikely items. Other radios may have exposed frayed exposed wiring or an unusual and unpleasant odor. Such phenomena are common, particularly when the radio has been stored in an outside barn or garage. Squirrels, raccoons, rats, mice, mud wasps and other assorted wildlife can be quite adaptive in making an abandoned radio their home. The damage caused by such occupancy can be severe. If you come across such a set and are tempted to buy it, inspect it carefully. The observed superficial problems are a likely indication of more extreme internal destruction. It is wise in such instances to take the trouble to remove the chassis for careful inspection.

DAMAGED TRANSFORMER

A common problem found in AC powered radios, and one that may be costly to remedy, is that of the 'smoked' transformer. Caused by a short circuit or overload, usually from faulty aged internal electronic components, damage to the transformer necessitates its repair or replacement. Fortunately, such problems are often easy to spot. Look for smoke damage to the chassis and on the inside of the cabinet. Also look for black goo, which may have hardened over time, oozing from the transformer itself. If the transformer is damaged, a replacement is the first option. New transformers are available from a number of sources, however their variety is limited. One might try to find a junker radio or salvage dealer with a transformer of matching specs. Another alternative is repair, a tedious process in which the transformer is dismantled and then rewound with copper wire. Transformer replacement can cost $20-$100+ assuming you are lucky enough to find a replacement.

MISSING TUBES

Missing tubes are generally easy to replace, particularly amongst radios from this era. The resources are numerous. The internet is an excellent resource for buying tested used tubes and there are many reputable dealers. For new and NOS (new old stock) tubes, check with local repair shops, mail order companies and specialty houses. It is a good idea to know your resources when considering the purchase of radio tubes. Some early tubes can cost as much as $50-75 each, used and testing good. Also be aware that there are components known as ballast tubes which resemble metal cased tubes superficially and plug into tube sockets, but which are actually resistors. From the author's experience, you can count on 50% of found ballast tubes needing replacement. Unlike filament tubes, few ballast tube NOS has survived and there are no known current resources for newly produced or good used components. Thus, replacing a failed ballast will require much perseverance or rewiring.

KNOBS

If one or more knobs are missing from a radio its value will be diminished. The purchaser of such a radio must resolve himself to either completing the set or substituting another complete set that looks aesthetically correct. If you chose to complete the set with correct knobs, you can either search for a replacement at swap meets or through a salvage dealer at a cost of about $5 to $25 per knob, or purchase a reproduction, usually in the same price range. There is now a wide variety of reproduction vintage knob types available and stocked by many vendors, most are plastic castings, a few are turned wood. If you need a knob which is not available as reproduction, there are a few specialty vendors who will make a casting and reproduction from a sample knob provided. Cost for such knobs typically begins at $25. Regardless of how you decide to deal with the missing knob(s), the paying price for the radio should be reduced accordingly.

DIAL LENSES, CRYSTALS AND SCALES

Covering the dial area on most radios made after 1933 is a glass or plastic dial lens. There area a few vendors who will reproduce a plastic lens from the damaged original or tracing of the opening, at a cost of around $20. Round glass dial lenses, typically made from convex round pieces of glass can usually be replaced with a clock crystal of the same diameter. Check with local clock makers or enthusiasts. As an alternative, you may decide to replace the glass with a plastic one purchased from a vendor as previously mentioned.

Early celluloid and plastic dial scales often became brittle and cracked, breaking or chipping over time. Other dial scale damage includes discoloration, burns from pilot lamps and human markings from overzealous DXers. Thankfully there is now a resource for replacing most any dial. Rock-Sea Enterprises, listed in the resource section of this book, is the only dedicated dial reproduction resource of which the author is aware. They produce an excellent product at a reasonable price. They inventory hundreds of scales and can custom make one they don't stock from what remains of your damaged scale. Rock-Sea also produces the widest variety of reproduction decals available.

BACKS

Most radios pictured in this book had backs when they were originally sold. Most don't now. The backs were typically flimsy cardboard which became worn and fell off never to be seen again. Often times the antenna was attached to the missing back and is now also missing. To most collectors the absence of a cardboard back will not detract from the value of a radio. Conversely, the presence of a back, particularly if it is in good condition, will add value. One exception to this rule are those radios made during the mid to late 1930's with molded plastic backs (like the Fada 260 series or the Emerson 199). With these radios the back is considered to be a critical element of the radio design and, as such, its absence can devalue a set by as much as 25%.

COLLECTORS' RESOURCES

As the hobby of vintage radio collecting has evolved and expanded over the years so have the resources for collectors. There are regional, national and international clubs. Cottage industries have developed, offering a wide range of products and services. Newsletters, bulletins, references books and monthly periodicals abound. Most recently, we have benefited from the proliferation of the internet.

With the popularization of the internet, shopping and resourcing for the hobbyist has become both easier and more convenient. With little knowledge and any search engine, you can locate hundreds of radio related web sites and find resources for club meetings, supplies, restoration techniques, and other enthusiasts to 'chat' with. A great place to start looking would be one of the web sites listed in the following Resource Listings pages of this book. Visit a site and browse the links page to locate other related sites and resources.

In addition to hobby-specific web sites, there are now several on-line auction houses, the largest of which, eBay, has become the primary forum for sales of vintage radios, parts, manuals and related memorabilia. On-line auctions have had a significant impact on the vintage radio hobby, as with all collectibles, decreasing the number of radios showing up at club meets, antique stores and shows. Only recently has this trend begun to reverse as a plethora of negative experinces have lured collectors back to the great outdoors. While the internet is an excellent resource, it lacks the social component that makes a hobby fun. While I continue to encourage collectors to spend time browsing auction, dealer and enthusiast sites, I maintain that the heart of this hobby remains in radio clubs at their meets and other functions.

NOTE: *Efforts have been made to verify information presented as accurate. Listings and accompanying information have been gathered as a resource for the collector and are not meant as an endorsement.*

RESOURCE LISTINGS

RADIOSWAPMEET.COM
MULTI-FACETED WEBSITE FOR VINTAGE RADIO
ENTHUSIASTS. INCLUDES RADIO CLUBS AND
ORANIZATIONS, FORUM AREA, PHOTO GALLERY,
RESTORATION TIPS, ARTICLES, TUBE EXCHANGE ,
SCHEMATICS.

ANTIQUE RADIO CLASSIFIED
WWW.ANTIQUERADIO.COM
PO BOX 802-V154, CARLISLE, MA 01741.
978-371-0512, ARC@ANTIQUERADIO.COM
LARGEST ANTIQUE RADIO MONTHLY MAGAZINE.
ARTICLES, CLASSIFIEDS & CLUB CALENDARS.
CALL OR WRITE FOR A FREE SAMPLE COPY.

ANTIQUE AUDIO
MARK OPPAT, BLANCHE STREET, PLYMOUTH, MI 48170
734-455-4169, 734-20-RADIO, MOPPAT@COMCAST.NET
RADIO & PHONOGRAPH PARTS, TUBES, REPAIR AND
RESTORATION SUPPLIES

ANTIQUE ELECTRONIC SUPPLY
WWW.TUBESANDMORE.COM
6221 SO. MAPLE AVENUE, TEMPE, AZ 85283
480-820-5411 , FAX 800-706-6789
RADIO & PHONOGRAPH PARTS, TUBES, REPAIR AND
RESTORATION SUPPLIES

DON DIERS
4276 N. 50TH STREET, MILWAUKEE, WI 53216
TUBES, CAPACITORS, GRILLE CLOTH, KNOBS,
KNOB FELTS, PUSHBUTTONS

GREAT NORTHERN ANTIQUES
WWW.GN4RADIOS.COM
5200 BLOOMINGTON AVENUE S, MINN., MN 55417
612-727-2489, FAX 612-824-3600, MTE612@AOL.COM
RADIO & PHONOGRAPH PARTS, TUBES, REPAIR AND
RESTORATION SUPPLIES, LITERATURE, SALVAGED PARTS
SPECIALIZING IN ZENITH AND EH SCOTT PARTS

THE NEW TUBE CO., WWW.NEWTUBE.COM
PO BOX 1243, VALLEY STREAM, NY 11582
PHONE+FAX 516-295-0390, INFO@NEWTUBE.COM
TUBES, CAPACITORS, GRILLE CLOTH, HANDLES, POTEN-
TIOMETERS, SPEAKER RECONE KITS

PLAY THINGS OF PAST
WWW.OLDRADIOPARTS.COM
2324 FAWN HAVEN DRIVE, MEDINA, OH 44256
330-558-0247, GBSPTOP@AOL.COM,
TUBES, RADIO & PHONOGRAPH PARTS, LITERATURE,
SALVAGED PARTS

RADIO DAZE
WWW.RADIODAZE.COM
7620 OMNITECH PLACE, VICTOR, NY 14564
585-742-2020, INFO@RADIODAZE.COM
TUBES, RADIO & PHONOGRAPH PARTS, TOOLS, REFIN-
ISHING SUPPLIES, GRILLE CLOTH

A. G. TANNENBAUM
WWW.AGTANNENBAUM.COM
PO BOX 386, AMBLER, PA 19002
215-657-0106, FAX 215-657-0520,
CUSTSERVE@AGTANNENBAUM.COM
MANUFACTURERS' MANUALS

ANTIQUE RADIOS, INC.
WWW.ARBEIII.COM
DAVID & NANCY SNOW, BOX 6352, JACKSON, MI 49204
517-787-2985
BATTERY ELIMINATORS

BAVARIAN RADIO WORKS
40 WALNUT ST., WHITMAN, MA 02382
781-447-4299 , BAVARIANRADIO@ATTBI.COM
EUROPEAN RADIO PARTS, REPAIR AND RESTORATION

BOB'S ANTIQUE RADIO & ELECTRONICS
WWW.RADIOANTIQUES.COM
111 E. 29TH ST., LA GRANGE PARK, IL 60526
708-352-0648, FAX 708-353-0647
RADIOBOB1@SBCGLOBAL.NET
CAPACITORS, PILOT LAMPS, AC POWER CORDS, DIAL
CORD, PLASTIC POLISHES

GARY BROWN TRANSFORMER REWINDING
478 FOREST AVE., ORONO, ME 04473
207-942-5745, GKBROWN@GWI.NET
TRANSFORMER REWINDING

CAYCE VINTAGE SOUND COMPANY
SCOTT MCAULEY, 117 SANDY LANE, CAYCE, SC 29033
803-791-0733, CAVISCO@AOL.COM
LEATHERETTE

CONSTANTINE WOOD CENTER
WWW.CONSTANTINES.COM
1040 E. OAKLAND PK BLVD, FT. LAUDERDALE, FL 33334
954-561-1716, INFO@CONSTANTINES.COM
REFINISHING SUPPLIES, VENEER

BARRY DAGESTINO
WWW.CROSLEYRADIOS.COM/SWAPSHOP-BARRY.HTML
1040 S HIDDEN CANYON RD, ANAHEIM HILLS, CA 92807
714-281-5190, DAGFAMILY@HOTMAIL.COM
CROSLEY NEW BUDDY & BUDDY BOY REPRO PARTS

PETER W. DAHL CO.
5869 WAYCROSS AVE., EL PASO, TX 79924
915-751-2300, FAX 915-751-0768, PWDCO@PWDAHL.COM
TRANSFORMER REWINDING

DAILY ELECTRONICS
WWW.WORLDACCESSNET.COM/~DAILY/DAILY.HTML
10914 NE 39TH STREET, #B-6, VANCOUVER, WA 98682
800-346-6667, DAILY@WORLDACCESSNET.COM
TUBES

DH DISTRIBUTORS
PO BOX 48623, WICHITA, KS 67201
PHONE & FAX 1-888-684-0050
CUSTOM MADE MULTI-SECTION ELECTROLYTICS

ELECTRON TUBE ENTERPRISES
MEMBERS.AOL.COM/ETETUBES/
BOX 8311, ESSEX, VT 05451
802-879-1844, FAX 802-870-7764, ETETUBES@GWI.NET
TUBES, BALLASTS, SCHEMATICS

FAIR RADIO SALES CO.
WWW.FAIRRADIO.COM
2395 ST. JOHNS ROAD, LIMA, OH 45802
419-227-6573, FAIRRADIO@FAIRRADIO.COM
TUBES, MILITARY SURPLUS ELECTRONICS

FRONTIER CAPACITOR
P.O.BOX 218, 403 S. MCINTOSH ST., LEHR, ND 58460
877-372-2341, FAX 701-378-2551
CAPACITORS, CAPACITOR REBUILDING

GARAGE-A-RECORDS
WWW.GARAGE-A-RECORDS.COM
11695 N. PIED PIPER PARKWAY, CROMWELL, IN 46732
219-856-4868, FAX 219-856-3620,
PHONOGRAPH PARTS & SUPPLIES

GEORGE H. FATHAUER
WWW.FATHAUER.COM
688 W. FIRST ST. #4, TEMPE, AZ 85281 ,
480-921-9961, FAX 480-921-9957, FATHAUER@COX.NET
COLLECTOR AND PRE-OCTAL TUBES, TUBE LITERATURE

KRIS GIMMY
1441 NOTTINGHAM DRIVE, AIKEN, SC 29801
803-649-9795, KRISGIMMY@EARTHLINK.NET
REPRO CATALIN BEZELS, GRILLES, HANDLES AND KNOBS

GRILLE CLOTH HQ
WWW.GRILLECLOTH.COM
624 CEDAR HILL ROAD, SUITE 100, AMBLER, PA 19002
JOHN@GRILLECLOTH.COM
REPRODUCTION GRILLE CLOTH

OLD TIME REPLICATIONS
WWW.ANTIQUERADIOKNOBS.COM
5744 TOBIAS AVENUE, VAN NUYS, CA 91411
818-786-2500, OLDTIMEREP@AOL.COM
REPRODUCTION BAKELITE, PLASKON & CATALIN PARTS

DICK OLIVER
1725 JUNIPER PLACE #310, GOSHEN, IN 46526
574-537-3747, DOLIVEARS@AOL.COM
REPRODUCTION PARTS FOR EARLY PHILCOS

RADIO ELECTRIC SUPPLY
WWW.VACUUMTUBES.NET
3500-R NW 97TH BL., GAINESVILLE, FL 32606
352-332-8881, TUBES@MINDSPRING.COM
TUBES

RADIO ERA ARCHIVES
RADIOERA.COM
2043 EMPIRE CENTRAL, DALLAS, TX 75235
214-358-5195, FAX 214-357-4693, TSM@RADIOERA.COM
LITERATURE, SCHEMATICS, MANUALS

DOYLE ROBERTS
305 N. CEDAR, MORRILTON, AR 72110
501-977-1861, DROBERTS30@TCWORKS.NET
REPRODUCTION PLASTIC DIAL COVERS

ROCK-SEA ENTERPRISES
MEMBERS.AOL.COM/ROCKSEAENT
PMB 241, 323-110 E. MATILIJA ST., OJAI, CA 93023
805-646-7362, DIALS@JUNO.COM
REPRODUCTION DIAL SCALES AND DECALS

THE TUBE SHOP
WWW.TUBE-SHOP.COM
BOX 231160, BOSTON, MA 02123
617-369-0980, TUBESHOP@QUICK.COM
TUBES

TUBE WORLD INC.
WWW.TUBEWORLD.COM
2712 SUPERIOR AVE., SHEBOYGAN, WI 53081
920-208-0353, TEKMAN@TUBEWORLD.COM
TUBES

STEVEN D. TURNER
WWW.CATALINRADIO.COM
5443 SCHULTZ DR., SYLVANIA, OH 43560
419-283-8203, SALES@CATALINRADIO.COM
REPRO AND VINTAGE CATALIN RADIO PARTS,
PLASTIC REFINISHING SUPPLIES

VACUUM TUBES, INC.
WWW.VACUUMTUBESINC.COM
10995-2A STATE RTE 128, HARRISON, OH 45030
513-738-8823, JIM@VACUUMTUBESINC.COM
TUBES, ADAPTERS, BALLASTS, DIAL LAMPS,
LITERATURE & SCHEMATICS

VINTAGE ELECTRONICS
WWW.VINTAGE-ELECTRONICS.COM
PO BOX 436, FALLSTON, MD 21047
VINTEL@COMCAST.NET
SALVAGED RADIO PARTS

OUTSIDER STUDIOS
5443 SCHULTZ DR., SYLVANIA, OH 43560
419-283-8203, OUTSIDERSTUDIOS@AOL.COM
PLASTIC & CATALIN RESTORATION AND REPAIR

PAUL PONTRELLO'S CATALIN RADIO REPAIR
WWW.HALCYON.COM/SMILES/REPAIRS.HTML
20205 11TH DR. SE, BOTHELL, WA 98012
425-345-6083, SMILES@HALCYON.COM
CATALIN RESTORATION AND REPAIR

TOPPO RESTORATIONS
WWW.RADIOATTIC.COM/ATTIC.PHP?SELLERID=26
5127 W. KINGS AVENUE, GLENDALE, AZ 88206
602-439-3556, LYNNTOPPO@EARTHLINK.NET
WOOD CABINET REPAIR AND RESTORATION

ALL SPEAKER REPAIR
3388 MERLIN ROAD, #300, GRANTS PASS, OR 97526
541-956-1803, DEEPCAVITY@HIGHSTREAM.NET
SPEAKER REPAIR

HANK BRAZEAL
3850 GALLERIA WOODS DRIVE #8, HOOVER, AL 35244
205-403-6243, HANKSPKR@CHARTER.NET
SPEAKER REPAIR

KEN GOODING
TWIN FALLS, IDAHO
208-734-2621, GOODGUYY@WEBTV.NET
SPEAKER REPAIR

JACKSON SPEAKER SERVICE
217 CRESTBROOK DR., JACKSON, MI 49203
517-789-6400

NEAL'S SPEAKER SERVICE
WWW.NEALSPEAKERREPAIR.COM
9300 MATADOR WAY, SACRAMENTO, CA 95826
916-363-6524, NEALSPEAKERS2@MSN.COM
SPEAKER REPAIR

ORANGE COUNTY SPEAKER
WWW.SPEAKERREPAIR.COM
12141 MARINERS WAY, GARDEN GROVE, CA 92843
800-897-8373, QUESTIONS@SPEAKERREPAIR.COM
SPEAKER REPAIR

SOUND REMEDY
331 VIRGINIA AVE., COLLINGSWOOD, NJ 08108
856-869-0238, FAX 856-869-6880
SPEAKER REPAIR

RUBEN ALHADEFF
WWW.SPEAKERREPAIRSERVICE.COM
521 E. PALM AVE., UNIT E, BURBANK, CA 91501
818- 232-1871, RUBEN@SPEAKERREPAIRSERVICE.COM
SPEAKER REPAIR

ANTIQUE RADIO CLUB LISTINGS
UNITED STATES AND CANADA

By far the best part of the hobby is meeting and spending time with other collectors. Club meets provide a forum for exchange of information, purchase of resources and new radio acquisitions. There are few collectors in the North America who are not within a few hours drive from a local or regional club.

Following is a listing of vintage radio clubs and related organizations throughout the United States and Canada:

NATIONAL

Antique Wireless Association (AWA)
PO Box 108, Stafford, NY 14816
www.antiquewireless.org

REGIONAL & LOCAL:

Alabama Historical Radio Society (ALHRS)
PO Box 26452, Birmingham, AL 35226
www.bham.net/ahrs/historicalradio@aol.org

Antique Radio Club of Illinois (ARCI)
PO Box 1139, LaGrange Park, IL 60526.
www.antique-radios.org.

Antique Radio Collectors Club of Ft. Smith,
Arkansas (ARCC)
4700 N. "N" St., Fort Smith, AR 72904

Antique Radio Collectors & Historians (ARCH)
of Greater St. Louis
2937 Raw Wind Dr., High Ridge, MO 63049
www.archradioclub.org

Antique Radio Collectors of Ohio (ARCO)
2929 Hazelwood Ave., Dayton, OH 45419

Arkansas Antique Radio Club (AARC)
PO Box 191117, Little Rock, AR 72219

Arizona Antique Radio Club (AARC)
2025 E. LaJolla Dr., Tempe, AZ 85282-5910

Belleville Area Antique Radio Club (BAARC)
4 Cresthaven Dr., Belleville, IL 62221

Border Amateur Radio Club
PO Box 372, Derby, VT 05829

Buckeye Antique Radio and Phonograph Club
1716 Chestnut Blvd., Cuyahoga Falls, OH 44223

California Historical Radio Society (CHRS)
PO Box 31659, San Francisco, CA 94131
www.californiahistoricalradio.com

CHRS/Sacramento Chapter (CHRS)
PO Box 162612, Sacramento, CA 95816-9998

Carolinas Chapter/AWA (CC-AWA)
PO Box 3015, Matthews, NC 28106
www.cc-awa.org

Central Ohio Antique Radio Assn (COARA)
3782 Mill Stream Dr., Hilliard, OH 43026
members.tripod.com/~COARA/index.htm

Central Pa. Radio Collectors Club
1045 Bonair Dr., Williamsport, PA 17701

Cincinnati Antique Radio Society
6 Indian Dr., Sardinia, OH 45171

Colorado Radio Collectors (CRC)
1058 Colt Cir., Castle Rock, CO 80109

Cumberland Valley Radio Society (CVRS)
HC-66, Box 1604, Barbourville, KY 40906

Delaware Valley Historic Radio Club (DVHRC)
PO Box 5053, New Britain, PA 18901
www.dvhrc.org

East Carolina Antique Radio Club (ECARC)
218 Bent Creek Dr., Greenville, NC 27834

Florida Antique Wireless Group (FAWG)
Box 738, Chuluota, FL 32766
www.clge.com/radiorelics/fawg.html

Greater Boston Antique Radio Collectors
c/o A.R.C., PO Box 2-W20, Carlisle, MA 01741

Greater New York Vintage Wireless Association
52 Uranus Rd., Rocky Point, NY 11778

Heartland Antique Radio Association (HLARA)
620 Fort Spunky Rd., Catoosa, OK 74015
www.hlara.org

Houston Vintage Radio Association (HVRA)
PO Box 31276, Houston, TX 77231
www.hvra.org

Hudson Valley Antique Radio and Phonograph
Society-AWA (HARPS)
PO Box 207, Campbell Hall, NY 10916

Indiana Historical Radio Society (IHRS)
245 N. Oakland Ave., Indianapolis, IN 46201
www.indianahistoricalradio.org

Illinois Historical Radio Society (IHRS)
8592 N. Creek Rd., Roscoe, IL 61073

Iowa Antique Radio Club and Historical Society
www.iarchs.org

Jacksonville Antique Radio Society (JARS)
www.jarsradioclub.com

Louisiana & Gulf Coast Antique Radio Club
750 Moore St., Baton Rouge, LA 70806

Memphis Antique Radio Club
459 Second St., Henderson, TN 38340
marc_memphisantiqueradioclub@hotmail.com

Michigan Antique Radio Club (MARC)
www.michiganantiqueradio.org

Mid-America Antique Radio Club
12309 W. 70th Terr., Shawnee, KS 66216
www.geocities.com/maarc1974

Mid-Atlantic Antique Radio Club (MAARC)
PO Box 352 Washington, VA 22747-0352
www.maarc.org

Mid-South Antique Radio Collectors (MSARC)
2479 W. Bluelick Rd, Shepardsville, KY 40165

Nashville Vintage Radio Club (NVRC)
5026 Suter Dr., Nashville, TN 37211
www.nashvillewebreview.com/radio/

Nebraska Antique Radio Collectors Club
905 West First, North Platte, NE 69101

New England Antique Radio Club (NEARC)
PO Box 122, Bradford, NH 03221
www.nearc.net

New Jersey Antique Radio Club (NJARC)
13 Cornell Pl., Manalapan, NJ 07726
www.njarc.org

New Mexico Radio Collectors Club (NMRCC)
39 Chaco Loop, Sandia Park, NM 87047
members.aol.com/NMRCC

Niagara Frontier Wireless Association (NFWA)
135 Autumnwood, Cheektowaga, NY 14227

Northland Antique Radio Club (NARC)
PO Box 18362, Minneapolis, MN 55418
www.geocities.com/TelevisionCity/4544/

Northwest Vintage Radio Society (NWVRS)
PO Box 82379, Portland, OR 97282-0379
nwvrs.org

Oklahoma Vintage Radio Collectors Club
Oklahoma City Chapter
PO Box 50625, Midwest City, OK 73140
members.cox.net/okvrc/

Pittsburgh Antique Radio Society, Inc. (PARS)
913 - 5th Ave. Patton, PA 16668
www.pittantiqueradios.org

Puget Sound Antique Radio Association
PO Box 2095, Snohomish, WA 98291
www.eskimo.com/~hhagen/psara

Radio Enthusiasts of Puget Sound (REPS)
14911 Linden N., Seattle, WA 98133
www.repsonline.org

Radio History Society, Inc. (RHS)
1205 Gladstone Dr., Rockville, MD 20851
www.radiohistory.org

Roanoke Antique Radio Enthusiasts (RARE)
3819 Bloonsboro Rd., Lynchburg, VA 24503

Schenectady Antique Radio Club (SARC)
Bldg. 20, Apt. 1, Corliss Park, Troy, NY12182
dadellers.tripod.com

Society for the Preservation of Antique
Radio Knowledge
PO Box 482, Dayton, OH 45449
www.antiqueradios.com/spark

Society of Wireless Pioneers
PO Box 86, Geyserville, CA 95441

South Florida Antique Radio Collectors
1717 N. Bayshore Dr., #1237, Miami, FL 33132

Southeastern Antique Radio Society (SARS)
113 Laurel Ridge Dr., Alpharetta, GA 30004
www.sarsradio.com

Southern California Antique Radio Fest
17665-1/4 Sierra Hwy, Canyon Country, CA 91351
home.pacbell.net/philbert/scarf/scarf.htm

Southern CA Antique Radio Society (SCARS)
9301 Texhoma Ave., Northridge, CA 91325
AntiqueRadios.org

Southern Vintage Wireless Association (SVWA)
8224 Bailey Cove Rd SE, #9, Huntsville, AL 35802

Texas Antique Radio Club (TARC)
218 Shannon Lee, San Antonio, TX 78216
www.gvtc.com/~edengel/TARC.htm

Texas Panhandle Vintage Radio Society (TPVRS)
4086 Business Park Dr., Amarillo, TX 79110

Tidewater Antique Radio Association (TARA)
7 Hillcrest Cir., Hampton, VA 23666

Tri-State Antique Radio Club
Box 172, Valley Cottage, NY 10989

Vintage Radio & Phonograph Society (VRPS)
PO Box 165345, Irving, TX 75016
www.vrps.org

W. Va. Chapter, AWA (AWA-WVC)
405 8th Ave., St. Albans, WV 25177

Wisconsin Antique Radio Club (WARC)
10230 W. Greenwood Ter., Milwaukee, WI 53224

CANADIAN CLUBS

NATIONAL:

Canadian Vintage Radio Society (CVRS)
4895 Mahood Dr., Richmond, BC V7E 5C3
www.canadianvintageradio.com

REGIONAL & LOCAL:

Alberta Chapter/CVRS
9611 142 St., Edmonton, Alberta T5N 2M8

British Columbia Chapter/CVRS
4895 Mahood Dr., Richmond, B.C. V7E 5C3

Manitoba Chapter/CVRS
3216 Assiniboine Ave
Winnipeg, Manitoba R3K 0B1

New Brunswick Chapter/CVRS
17 Maple Crescent
Rothesay, New Brunswick E2E 2A4

Newfoundland Chapter/CVRS
11 Gulliver, St. John's, Newfoundland A1E 4K5

Nova Scotia Chapter/CVRS
4 Baird St., North Sydney, Nova Scotia B2A 2B3

Ontario Chapter/CVRS
79 Meadowlands Dr., Nepean, Ontario K2G 2R9

Saskatchewan Chapter/CVRS
Box 174, Melfort, Saskatchewan S0E 1A0

Yukon and NWT Chapter/CVRS
21 Hyland Cres., Whitehorse, Yukon Y1A 4P6

Range Land Collecting Club
912 7A St. S, Lethbridge, Alberta T1J 2J2

Society for the Preservation of Antique Radio
220- 4411 Hastings St. E, Burnaby, BC V5C 2K1.
www.bc.sympatico.ca/radiomuseum

London Vintage Radio Club (LVRC)
42 Clematis Rd., North York
Ontario, Canada M2J 4X2
www.lvrc.homestead.com/index.html

Ottawa Vintage Radio Club (OVRC)
Box 84084, Ottawa, Ontario K2C 3Y9
www.ovrc.org

Quebec Society for Vintage Radio Collectors
SQCRA, 224 Decelles, Brigham
Quebec, Canada J2K 4S5
www.sqcra.qc.ca/maindex.html

*Club listings have been provided courtesy
of Antique Radio Classified, antique radio's
largest circulation monthly magazine.
Articles, classifieds & club calendars.
Call or write for a free sample copy.*

*Antique Radio Classified
PO Box 802-V154
Carlisle, MA 01741.
978-371-0512, Fax: 978-371-7129.
www.antiqueradio.com*

LEGEND

The following pages comprise the identification and price guide section of this reference. All listings are arranged alphabetically by manufacturer and then numerically by model number within each manufacturer.

Each radio is pictured and described as follows:

1. SILVERTONE **2.** 6110 **3.** CA1938
2. 'ROCKET'
4. KARSTADT DESIGN
5. BAKELITE, **6.** 5 TUBES, **7.** 1 BAND
9. BROWN **10.** $1700, **9.** BLACK **10.** $2000

1. Manufacturer Brand Name
2. Model Number and/or Model Name
3. Approximate Year of Manufacture
4. Industrial Designer if known or attributed
5. Description of Cabinet Material(s)
6. Tube Count
7. Band Count
8. Special Features/Options
9. Model Variations (if any)
10. Current Market Value(s) Including Variants

ABC CA1960
STYRENE, 5 TUBES, 1 BAND
WHITE $40, PINK $75, BLUE $75

ACRATONE 201 CA1938
5 TUBES, 1 BAND
BROWN BAKELITE $225
IVORY PLASKON $350

ADDISON 55 CA1950
BAKELITE, 5 TUBES, 1 BAND
BROWN OR PAINTED $50

ADDISON 61 CA1953
BAKELITE, 4 TUBES, 1 BAND
BROWN OR PAINTED $40

ADDISON 63 CA1953
BAKELITE, 5 TUBES, 1 BAND
BROWN OR PAINTED $50

ADDISON 64 CA1953
BAKELITE, 6 TUBES, 1 BAND
BROWN OR PAINTED $65

ADDISON 2A, L2F CA1946-7
'BABY ADDISON'
5 TUBES, 1 BAND
BROWN BAKELITE $250
BLACK BAKELITE $300
MAROON BAKELITE $350
IVORY PLASKON $450
LT GREEN PLASKON $1200
LT BLUE PLASKON $1200
MAROON BAKELITE+IVORY PLASKON $750
BLUE-GREEN BEETLE+IVORY PLASKON $1200

ADDISON 2A CA1946-7
'BABY ADDISON'
CATALIN, 5 TUBES, 1 BAND
YELLOW+MAROON $1500
YELLOW+RED $1800
MAROON+YELLOW $1500
EBONY+YELLOW $2000

ADDISON 5A CA1942-7
'THEATRE'
CATALIN, 5 TUBES, 1 BAND
LT GREEN+MAROON $2500
LT GREEN+YELLOW $2500
MAROON+YELLOW $2200
EBONY+YELLOW $2500

ADMIRAL 4L-28 CA1959
STYRENE
$35

ADMIRAL 4R11 CA1951
STYRENE, 4 TUBES, 1 BAND
GREEN $60, RED $75, BLACK $50

ADMIRAL 5-J3 CA1952
STYRENE, 5 TUBES, 1 BAND
$40

ADMIRAL 5-Z22,23 CA1949
BAKELITE+ALUMINUM, 5 TUBES, 1 BAND
BROWN $25
BLACK $30
PAINTED IVORY $25

ADMIRAL 5A-32 CA1952
BAKELITE CABINET, METAL TRIM
5 TUBES, 1 BAND
BROWN $25, BLACK $30

ADMIRAL 5B4 CA1958
STYRENE, 5 TUBES, 1 BAND
$25

5D4 CA1958
STYRENE, 5 TUBES, 1 BAND
$25

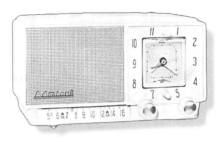

ADMIRAL 5E31-39 CA1954
STYRENE, 6 TUBES, 1 BAND
BLACK $25, BROWN $20, IVORY $25
GREEN 50, GRAY $25

ADMIRAL 5G31,32,332 CA1954
6 TUBES, 1 BAND
BAKELITE: BROWN $60, BLACK $75
PLASKON: IVORY $75

ADMIRAL 5J2 CA1951
BAKELITE, 5 TUBES, 1 BAND
BROWN OR PAINTED $25
BLACK $30

ADMIRAL 5S-21 CA1952
BAKELITE, 5 TUBES, 1 BAND
BROWN OR PAINTED $30
BLACK $45

ADMIRAL 5T31 CA1955
BAKELITE, 5 TUBES, 1 BAND
BROWN OR PAINTED $25
BLACK $30

ADMIRAL 5X-21 CA1952
BAKELITE, 5 TUBES, 1 BAND
BROWN OR PAINTED $25
BLACK $40

ADMIRAL 5Z-22 CA1952
BAKELITE+ALUMINUM, 5 TUBES, 1 BAND
BROWN OR PAINTED $40

ADMIRAL 6A22 CA1951
BAKELITE, 5 TUBES, 1 BAND
BROWN OR PAINTED $25
BLACK $30

ADMIRAL 6C-22 CA1952
BAKELITE WITH CHROME TRIM
BROWN OR PAINTED $50

ADMIRAL 6T-01 CA1946
BAKELITE, 5 TUBES, 1 BAND
BROWN OR PAINTED $25
BLACK $30

ADMIRAL 6T-02 CA1946
BAKELITE, 5 TUBES, 1 BAND
BROWN OR PAINTED $25
BLACK $30

7T10-5K1 CA1947
BAKELITE, 5 TUBES, 1 BAND
BROWN OR PAINTED $25
BLACK $30

ADMIRAL 7T12-4B1 CA1947
BAKELITE, 4 TUBES, 1 BAND, DC
BROWN $20

ADMIRAL 8SI CA1959
STYRENE, TRANSISTOR, 1 BAND, DC
$45

ADMIRAL 12-B5 CA1940
BAKELITE, 5 TUBES, 1 BAND
BAKELITE: BROWN $50, BLACK $60
IVORY PLASKON $75

ADMIRAL 15-D5 CA1941
5 TUBES, 1 BAND
BAKELITE: BROWN $125, BLACK $140
IVORY PLASKON $175

ADMIRAL 20-A6 CA1940
5 TUBES, 1 BAND
BAKELITE: BROWN $110, BLACK $125
IVORY PLASKON $150

ADMIRAL 48-J6,49-J6 CA1941
BAKELITE, 5 TUBES, 2 BANDS
BROWN $40
PAINTED IVORY $40

ADMIRAL 51-K6,52-K6 CA1941
BAKELITE, 5 TUBES, 2 BANDS
BROWN $40
PAINTED IVORY $40

ADMIRAL 113-5A CA1938
5 TUBES, 1 BAND
BAKELITE: BROWN $150, BLACK $175
IVORY PLASKON $250

ADMIRAL 125-5E 'JUNIOR' CA1938
4 TUBES, 1 BAND
BAKELITE: BROWN $100, BLACK $115
IVORY PLASKON $175, BEETLE $250

ADMIRAL 158-5J CA1939
4 TUBES, 1 BAND
BAKELITE: BROWN $100, BLACK $115
IVORY PLASKON $175, BEETLE $250

ADMIRAL 163-5L,389-5S CA1940
5 TUBES, 1 BAND
BAKELITE: BROWN $110, BLACK $125
IVORY PLASKON $150, BEETLE $250

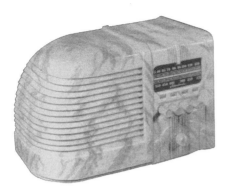

ADMIRAL 168-5D CA1939
5 TUBES, 1 BAND
BAKELITE: BROWN $150, BLACK $175
IVORY PLASKON $225, BEETLE $350

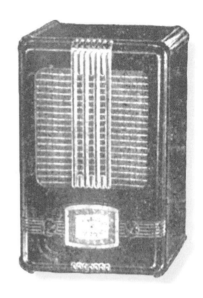

ADMIRAL 985-5Z, 990-5Z, 985-6Y, 990-6Y CA1938
5 TUBES, 1 BAND
BROWN BAKELITE $200, BLACK BAKELITE $250
IVORY PLASKON $325

ADMIRAL 361-5Q, 577-5Q CA1940
5 TUBES, 1 BAND
BAKELITE: BROWN $125, BLACK $150
IVORY PLASKON $225, BEETLE $300

**ADMIRAL
371-5R, 372-5R, 373-5R CA1940**
5 TUBES, 1 BAND
BAKELITE: BROWN $150, BLACK $175
IVORY PLASKON $225, BEETLE $350

ADMIRAL 990-6Y CA1938
6 TUBES, 2 BANDS
BROWN BAKELITE $200, BLACK BAKELITE $250
IVORY PLASKON $325

ADMIRAL
366-6J, 367-6J, 368-6J CA1941
5 TUBES, 1 BAND
BAKELITE: BROWN $150, BLACK $175
IVORY PLASKON $225, BEETLE $350IVORY 225,
BEETLE $450

ADMIRAL 512-6C CA1938
5 TUBES, 1 BAND
BROWN BAKELITE $75, BLACK BAKELITE $90
IVORY PLASKON $110516-5G+1 CA1938
5 TUBES, 1 BAND
516-5G BROWN BAKELITE $60
516-5I IVORY PLASKON $90

ADMIRAL 4202-B6 CA1941
5 TUBES, 1 BAND
BAKELITE: BROWN $50, BLACK $60
IVORY PLASKON $90, BEETLE $175

ADMIRAL PEE WEE CA1946
5 TUBES, 1 BAND
BAKELITE: BROWN $50, BLACK $75
PLASKON: IVORY $125, RED $350

AETNA 602 CA1940
BAKELITE, 6 TUBES, 2 BANDS
BROWN $200, BLACK $250

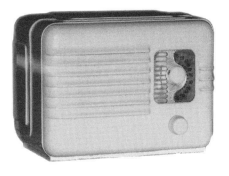

AETNA PEE WEE CA1939
4 TUBES, 1 BAND
BROWN BAKELITE $125
IVORY PLASKON $200

AIR CASTLE 287,328 CA1947
BAKELITE, 5 TUBES, 1 BAND
BROWN OR PAINTED $50

AIR CASTLE 300,325 CA1947
5 TUBES, 1 BAND
BROWN BAKELITE $50
IVORY PLASKON $75

AIR CASTLE 314 CA1951
BAKELITE, 4 TUBES, 1 BAND
BROWN OR PAINTED $45

AIR CASTLE 315,316, 1951
BAKELITE, 5 TUBES, 1 BAND
BROWN OR PAINTED $20

AIR CASTLE 317,8 1951
BAKELITE, 5 TUBES, 1 BAND
BROWN OR PAINTED $30

AIR CASTLE 383 CA1951
BAKELITE, 8 TUBES, AM-FM
BROWN OR PAINTED $110

AIR CASTLE 708 CA1951
BAKELITE+PLASKON, 5 TUBES, 1 BAND
BLACK+IVORY $75

AIR CASTLE 2006, 7 CA1940
BAKELITE, 5 TUBES, 2 BANDS
BROWN OR PAINTED $50

AIR CASTLE 7108,9 CA1939
4 TUBES, 1 BAND, AC-DC
BROWN BAKELITE $225
IVORY PLASKON $350

AIR CASTLE 7110,11,12 CA1939
6 TUBES, 1 BAND
BAKELITE: BROWN $90
PLASKON: IVORY $125, BEETLE $275

AIR CHIEF PATRIOT CA1942
6 TUBES, 2 BANDS
RED, WHITE+BLUE PAINTED BAKELITE
$150

AIR KING 222 CA1939
4 TUBES, 1 BAND
BAKELITE: BROWN $50, BLACK $70
IVORY PLASKON $125

AIR KING A400 CA1947
4 TUBES, 1 BAND
BAKELITE: BROWN $50, BLACK $70
IVORY PLASKON $125

AIR KING A-511 CA1950
5 TUBES, 1 BAND
BROWN BAKELITE $50
IVORY PLASKON $90

**AIR KING A600 CA1946
'DUCHESS'**

CATALIN, 5 TUBES, 1 BAND
GREEN+YELLOW $1500
MAROON+YELLOW $1200
YELLOW+GREEN $1200
YELLOW+MAROON $1200

**AIR KING A600 CA1946
'DUCHESS'**

STYRENE, 8 TUBES AM-FM
BLACK+IVORY STYRENE WITH
ALABASTER CATALIN KNOBS $600

AIR KING 52 CA1933
'EGYPTIAN'

AIR KING 66 CA1933
'GLOBES' OR 'CLOCK'

HAROLD VAN DOREN DESIGN
5 TUBES, 1 BAND
BAKELITE: BLACK $4,000, BLACK+CRYSTAL FINISH $5,000, BROWN $2,000
PLASKON: IVORY $3,000, IVORY+CRYSTAL FINISH $4,500 LT PURPLE $8,000
LT BLUE $8,000, LT GREEN $8,000, RED $12,000

AIR KING 72 CA1933
'SKYSCRAPER'
5 TUBES, 1 BAND
BAKELITE: BLACK $3000, BROWN $2500
BLACK+CRYSTALLINE FINISH $3500
PLASKON: IVORY $3500,BLUE $6000
GREEN $6000, LAVENDER $6000
RED $8000

AIR KING 770 CA1937
'CYCLOPS'
'FLOUNDER'
6 TUBES,1 BAND
BAKELITE: BROWN $750, BLACK $1200
PLASKON: IVORY $1500, RED $3500

AIR KING A520 CA1948
4 TUBES, 1 BAND
BAKELITE: BROWN $50, BLACK $75, RED $90
IVORY PLASKON $90

AIRLINE 386,636 CA1937
6 TUBES, 1 BAND
BAKELITE: BLACK $175, BROWN $150
IVORY PLASKON $225

AIRLINE 320 CA1939
5 TUBES, 1 BAND
BAKELITE: BLACK $125, BROWN $100
IVORY PLASKON $150

AIRLINE 350 CA1938
5 TUBES, 1 BAND
BAKELITE: BLACK $175, BROWN $150
IVORY PLASKON $250

AIRLINE 420 CA1940
4 TUBES, 1 BAND
BAKELITE: BLACK $100, BROWN $75
PAINTED RED, GREEN OR WHITE $90

AIRLINE 355 CA1938
5 TUBES, 1 BAND
BAKELITE: BLACK $200, BROWN $175
IVORY PLASKON $250

AIRLINE 465 CA1938
6 TUBES, 1 BAND
BAKELITE: BLACK $175, BROWN $150
IVORY PLASKON $225

AIRLINE 458 CA1939
BAKELITE, 4 TUBES, 1 BAND, DC
BROWN OR PAINTED $75

AIRLINE 501 CA1939
5 TUBES, 1 BAND
BAKELITE: BLACK $150, BROWN $135
IVORY PLASKON $200

AIRLINE 508 CA1939
BAKELITE, 5 TUBES, 1 BAND
BROWN OR PAINTED $125

AIRLINE 420,511,1501 CA1941
BAKELITE, 4 TUBES, 1 BAND
5 TUBES, 1 BAND
BROWN OR PAINTED BAKELITE $75

AIRLINE 513B CA1947
BAKELITE, 5 TUBES, 1 BAND
BROWN OR PAINTED $75

AIRLINE 513 CA1941
BAKELITE, 5 TUBES, 1 BAND
BROWN OR PAINTED $90

518, 519 CA1942
BAKELITE, 5 TUBES, 1 BAND
BROWN OR PAINTED $75

AIRLINE 525 CA1941
BAKELITE, 5 TUBES, 1 BAND
BROWN OR PAINTED $125

350,604 CA1938
6 TUBES, 1 BAND
BROWN OR PAINTED BAKELITE $250
IVORY PLASKON $350

AIRLINE 602 CA1938
BAKELITE, 6 TUBES, 1 BAND
BROWN OR PAINTED $175

AIRLINE 734 CA1942
BAKELITE, 7 TUBES, 2 BANDS
BROWN OR PAINTED $125
BLACK+RED MARBLE $225

AIRLINE 610 CA1941
BAKELITE, 6 TUBES, 1 BAND
BROWN OR PAINTED $75

AIRLINE 624,255 CA1940
BAKELITE, 6 TUBES, 1 BAND
BROWN OR PAINTED $50

AIRLINE 1407, 1507 CA1939
5 TUBES, 1 BAND
BROWN OR PAINTED $225

AIRLINE 1503,1525 CA1948
5 TUBES, 1 BAND
BROWN OR PAINTED $25

AIRLINE 1527,1553 CA1950
5 TUBES, 1 BAND
BROWN OR PAINTED $25

AIRLINE 1529 CA1950
BAKELITE, 7 TUBES, AM-FM
BROWN OR PAINTED $20

AIRLINE 1535 CA1950
BAKELITE, 7 TUBES, AM-FM
BROWN OR PAINTED $50

AIRLINE 1536 CA1950
BAKELITE, 5 TUBES, 1 BAND
BROWN OR PAINTED $60

AIRLINE 1542 CA1952
BAKELITE, 5 TUBES, 1 BAND
BROWN OR PAINTED $35

AIRLINE 1543 CA1952
BAKELITE, 5 TUBES, 1 BAND
BROWN OR PAINTED $15

AIRLINE 1548 CA1955
BAKELITE, 5 TUBES, 1 BAND
BROWN OR PAINTED $30

AIRLINE 1557 CA1955
BAKELITE, 5 TUBES, 1 BAND
BROWN OR PAINTED $35

AIRLINE 1564 CA1955
BAKELITE, 4 TUBES, 1 BAND
BROWN OR PAINTED $20

AIRLINE 1572 CA1955
BAKELITE, 8 TUBES, AM-FM
BROWN OR PAINTED $25

AIRLINE 1576 CA1958
BAKELITE, 4 TUBES, 1 BAND
BROWN OR PAINTED $25

AIRLINE 1577, 1578 CA1955
BAKELITE, 4 TUBES, 1 BAND
BROWN OR PAINTED $25

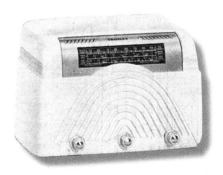

AIRLINE 1579, 1580 CA1950
BAKELITE, 5 TUBES, 3 BANDS
BROWN OR PAINTED $50

AIRLINE 1590, 1591, 1592 CA1950
BAKELITE, 5 TUBES, 1 BAND
BROWN OR PAINTED $65

AIRLINE 1615 CA1958
BAKELITE, 4 TUBES, 1 BAND
BROWN OR PAINTED $20

AIRLINE 1628 CA1959
STYRENE, 4 TUBES, 1 BAND
$20

AIRLINE 1637 CA1958
BAKELITE, 6 TUBES, 1 BAND
BLACK $15

AIRLINE 1638 CA1960
STYRENE, 6 TUBES, 1 BAND
TAN+IVORY $45, GRAY $25

AIRLINE 1645, 1646 CA1958
STYRENE, 6 TUBES, 1 BAND
GREEN $50, BROWN $20

AIRLINE 1653,1654 C1958
STYRENE, 6 TUBES, 1 BAND
IVORY $25, BLUE $65

AIRLINE 1655 CA1958
STYRENE, 4 TUBES, 1 BAND
BROWN $20, IVORY $25, PINK $50

AIRLINE 1660 CA1959
STYRENE, 5 TUBES, 1 BAND
IVORY+GREY $30, BLUE $50

AIRLINE 1662, 1670, 1850 CA1958
STYRENE, 5 TUBES, 1 BAND
IVORY $25, BLACK $20
BLUE $50, PINK $45

AIRLINE 1666 CA1960
STYRENE, 8 TUBES, AMFM
BROWN+IVORY $40

AIRLINE 1667 CA1960
STYRENE, 5 TUBES, 1 BAND
PINK+IVORY $75
RED+IVORY $90

AIRLINE 1673 CA1959
STYRENE, 5 TUBES, 1 BAND
BLACK $50, BROWN $25

ARIA 571 CA1946
STYRENE, 5 TUBES, 1 BAND
BLACK+IVORY $50

ARROW C57 CA1938
5 TUBES, 2 BANDS, AC-DC
BLACK BAKELITE $225
IVORY PLASKON $350

ARVIN 58 CA1939
BAKELITE, 5 TUBES, 1 BAND
BROWN OR PAINTED $110
BLACK $140

ARVIN 68 CA1939
BAKELITE, 5 TUBES, 1 BAND
BROWN OR PAINTED $125
BLACK $175

ARVIN 160 CA1948
BAKELITE, 5 TUBES, 1 BAND
BROWN OR PAINTED $20

ARVIN 241P CA1949
STYRENE, 4 TUBES, 1 BAND
IVORY $100

ARVIN 358T CA1950
BAKELITE, 5 TUBES, 1 BAND
BROWN OR PAINTED $60
BLACK $75

ARVIN 446P CA1950
STYRENE, 4 TUBES, 1 BAND
IVORY $75

ARVIN 450T CA1948
BAKELITE, 5 TUBES, 1 BAND
BROWN OR PAINTED $75

ARVIN 460T CA1953
STYRENE, 5 TUBES, 1 BAND
$25

ARVIN 253, 356 CA1950
KARSTADT DESIGN
BAKELITE, 4 TUBES, 1 BAND
BLACK $150, BROWN $90, IVORY $135

ARVIN 553T CA1951
BAKELITE, 5 TUBES, 1 BAND
BROWN OR PAINTED $65

ARVIN 532 CA1940

CATALIN, 5 TUBES, 1 BAND
MAROON+YELLOW $2,000
ONYX+TORTOISE $2,500

ARVIN 555 CA1946
5 TUBES, 1 BAND, AC-DC
BROWN OR PAINTED $25

ARVIN 616 CA1942
6 TUBES, 1 BAND, AC-DC
BROWN OR PAINTED $90
BLACK $125

ARVIN 651T CA1951
BAKELITE, 5 TUBES, 1 BAND
BROWN OR PAINTED $50

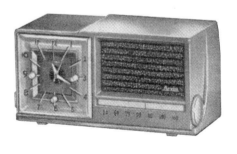

ARVIN 657T CA1951
BAKELITE, 5 TUBES, 1 BAND
BROWN OR PAINTED $40

ARVIN 664, 722 CA1941
BAKELITE, 6 TUBES, 1 BAND
BROWN OR PAINTED $40

ARVIN 741T CA1954
BAKELITE, 5 TUBES, 1 BAND
BROWN OR PAINTED $110

ARVIN 753T CA1954
BAKELITE, 5 TUBES, 1 BAND
BROWN OR PAINTED $95

ARVIN 758T CA1954
STYRENE, 5 TUBES, 1 BAND
$15

ARVIN 76OT CA1954
STYRENE, 5 TUBES, 1 BAND
$15

ARVIN 95OT CA1957
STYRENE, 5 TUBES, 1 BAND
BLACK $75, IVORY $80
GREEN $90

ARVIN 952P1 CA1955
STYRENE, 4 TUBES, 1 BAND
BLACK $40, IVORY $50
GREEN $60, RED $75

ARVIN 9562 CA1957
STYRENE, TRANSISTOR, 1 BAND
IVORY $50, BLUE $90

ARVIN 2564 CA1957
5 TUBES, 1 BAND
IVORY $40, BLACK $45

ARVIN 2572 CA1957
5 TUBES, 1 BAND
IVORY $70, GREEN $80
RED $125, AVOCADO $110

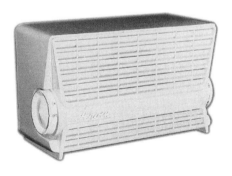

ARVIN 2581 CA1958
STYRENE, 5 TUBES, 1 BAND
IVORY $60, OLIVE $70, BLACK $110

ARVIN 3561 CA1957
6 TUBES, 1 BAND
IVORY $50, TAN $45

ARVIN 5571 CA1957
5 TUBES, 1 BAND
IVORY $75, GREEN $110

ARVIN 5561 CA1957
5 TUBES, 1 BAND
IVORY $45, PINK $80, MAROON $60

ARVIN 5578 CA1957
5 TUBES, 1 BAND
IVORY $40, RED $90

ARVIN 9574 CA1957
TRANSISTOR, AC-DC
TAN $45, IVORY $60

ARVIN RE267 CA1948
KARLSTADT DESIGN
STYRENE, 4 TUBES, 1 BAND
MARBLED $225

AUTOMATIC 440 CA1940
6 TUBES, 1 BAND
BROWN OR PAINTED BAKELITE $75
IVORY PLASKON $140

AUTOMATIC CA1936
BAKELITE, 5 TUBES, 1 BAND
BROWN $175

AUTOMATIC CA1934
'TOM THUMB JUNIOR'
BAKELITE, 5 TUBES, 1 BAND
BROWN $1200, BLACK $1500

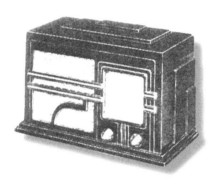

AUTOMATIC 8-15 CA1937
5 TUBES, 1 BAND
BAKELITE: BLACK $350,
PLASKON: IVORY $750, RED $1500
GREEN $1500

AUTOMATIC 601 CA1947
6 TUBES, 1 BAND
BROWN OR PAINTED BAKELITE $90

AUTOMATIC CA1939
5 TUBES, 1 BAND
BROWN OR PAINTED BAKELITE $75

AUTOMATIC 402 CA1940
5 TUBES, 1 BAND
BROWN OR PAINTED BAKELITE $100

AUTOMATIC 614X CA1946
BAKELITE, 6 TUBES, 1 BAND
BROWN OR PAINTED $75

BELMONT 116 CA1947
BAKELITE, 5 TUBES, 1 BAND
BROWN OR PAINTED $150

BELMONT 110 CA1947
BAKELITE, 6 TUBES, 1 BAND
BROWN OR PAINTED $75

BELMONT 111 CA1946
6 TUBES, 1 BAND
BAKELITE, 6 TUBES, 1 BAND
BROWN OR PAINTED $150

BELMONT 114 CA1947
5 TUBES, 1 BAND
BROWN OR PAINTED $160

BELMONT 115 CA1946
BAKELITE, 4 TUBES, 1 BAND, DC
BROWN OR PAINTED $200

BELMONT 117 CA1947
BAKELITE, 6 TUBES, 1 BAND
BROWN OR PAINTED $75

BELMONT 118 CA1938
4 TUBES, 1 BAND
BROWN OR PAINTED $200

BELMONT 128,534 CA1946
6 TUBES, 1 BAND
BROWN OR PAINTED $125

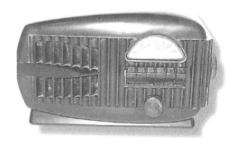

BELMONT 121 CA1946
BAKELITE, 6 TUBES, 1 BAND
BROWN OR PAINTED $150

BELMONT 510,518 CA1938
5 TUBES, 1 BAND
BROWN OR PAINTED $125

BELMONT 519,635 CA1939
5+6 TUBES, 1 BAND
BROWN OR PAINTED $375

BELMONT 526 'SCOTTY' CA1937
5 TUBES, 1 BAND
BAKELITE: BROWN $200, BLACK $225
IVORY PLASKON $325

BELMONT 602 'SCOTTY' CA1937
5 TUBES, 1 BAND
BAKELITE: BROWN $200, BLACK $225
IVORY PLASKON $325

BENDIX 65P4U CA1948
BAKELITE, 6 TUBES, 1 BAND
$25

BENDIX 55P2U,111 CA1948
BAKELITE,5 TUBES,1 BAND
$30

BENDIX 55P3U CA1948
BAKELITE,5 TUBES,1 BAND
$50

BENDIX 75P6U CA1949
BAKELITE,7 TUBES,AM-FM
$65

BENDIX 114 CA1948
STYRENE ,5TUBES, 1 BAND
MARBLED BROWN+TAN $550
MARBLED IVORY+MAROON $750

BENDIX 526 CA1946
CATALIN, 5TUBES, 1 BAND
MARBLED GREEN+BLACK $950

BENDIX 526D CA1946
BAKELITE, 5 TUBES, 1 BAND
$75

BENDIX 626C CA1946
BAKELITE, 6 TUBES, 2 BANDS
$50

BENDIX 953A CA1953
STYRENE, 5 TUBES, 1 BAND
$40

BLONDER-TONGUET-88 CA1959
STYRENE, 5 TUBES, 1 BAND
$40

BULOVA 100 CA1957
STYRENE, 5 TUBES, 1 BAND
AQUA $50, BLACK $40
PINK $75, WHITE $40

BULOVA 204 CA1955
STYRENE, 4 TUBES, 1 BAND
IVORY $50, BLACK $55
GREEN $65

BULOVA 300 CA1958
STYRENE, 5 TUBES, 1 BAND
AQUA $75, BLACK $60
PINK $75, WHITE $50

BULOVA CA1959
STYRENE, 5 TUBES, 1 BAND
AQUA $50, TAN $30
PINK $60

CAPEHART 2T55 CA1956
STYRENE, 5 TUBES, 1 BAND
$25

CAPEHART 3T55 CA1956
STYRENE, 5 TUBES, 1 BAND
$40

CAPEHART TC20, TC62 CA1953
STYRENE, 6 TUBES, 1 BAND
$40

CAPEHART T30 CA1952
STYRENE, 5 TUBES, 1 BAND
$40

CAPEHART T54 CA1954
STYRENE, 5 TUBES, 1 BAND
$25

CAPEHART T522 CA1953
STYRENE, 5 TUBES, 1 BAND
$50

CAPEHART TC500 CA1953
STYRENE, 6 TUBES, 1 BAND
$20

CAVALCADE RS1A CA1947
STYRENE, 4 TUBES, 1 BAND
MARBELED $175

COLUMBIA CA1935
BAKELITE, 5 TUBES, 1 BAND
$250

CBS 2160 CA1958
STYRENE, 5 TUBES, 1 BAND
IVORY $75, BLACK $95
GREEN $110

COLUMBIA+CBS 5158 CA1958
STYRENE, 5 TUBES, 1 BAND
IVORY $25, BLACK $35

CHANNEL MASTER 6511 CA1959
STYRENE, 4 TUBES, 1 BAND, DC
OLIVE $60, TAN $40

CHANNEL MASTER 6532 CA1958
STYRENE, 4 TUBES, 1 BAND, DC
IVORY+TAN $25

CLARION 402,502 CA1940
BAKELITE, 4,5 TUBES, 1 BAND
BROWN OR PAINTED $45

CLARION 11802 CA1948
BAKELITE, 5 TUBES, 1 BAND
BROWN OR PAINTED $50

COLONIAL 300 CA1933
5 TUBES, 1 BAND
BLACK BAKELITE+CHROME
$1200

CONTINENTAL 396 CA1940
6 TUBES, 2 BANDS
BAKELITE: BROWN $150
PLASKON: IVORY $225, BEETLE $375

CONTINENTAL 1600 CA1948
STYRENE, 5 TUBES, 1 BAND
IVORY $175, BLACK $175
YELLOW $400

CORONADO 43-8190 CA1947
BAKELITE, 5 TUBES, 1 BAND
IVORY+BLUE MARBLED TENITE TRIM $350

CORONADO 115 CA1953
BAKELITE, 5 TUBES, 1 BAND
BROWN OR PAINTED $25

CORONADO 'JEWEL' CA1938
BAKELITE, 4 TUBES, 1 BAND
BROWN OR PAINTED $175

CORONADO 391 CA1939
5 TUBES, 1 BAND
BROWN OR PAINTED $125

CROSLEY 5F 'GRADUATE' CA1955
PAINTED BAKELITE, 5 TUBES, 1 BAND
CHARTREUSE $70, IVORY $30
BROWN $25, RED $65

CROSLEY 9-103 CA1949
BAKELITE, 5 TUBES, 1 BAND
BROWN OR PAINTED IVORY $60

CROSLEY 9-113 CA1949
BAKELITE, 5 TUBES, 1 BAND
BROWN OR PAINTED IVORY $20

CROSLEY 9-118 CA1949
BAKELITE, 5 TUBES, 1 BAND
BROWN OR PAINTED IVORY $45

CROSLEY 9-119, C568A CA1949
'FIVER'
BAKELITE, 5 TUBES, 1 BAND
BROWN OR PAINTED IVORY $75

CROSLEY 10-127 CA1950
BAKELITE, 5 TUBES, 1 BAND
BROWN $65, ALMOND $75

CROSLEY 10-135 CA1950
PAINTED BAKELITE, 5 TUBES, 1 BAND
WHITE+CHROME $75, BLACK+GOLD $60
CHARTREUSE+GOLD $100, MAROON+GOLD $90
AQUA+CHROME $125, GREEN+CHROME $100

CROSLEY 11-100U CA1951
'BULLSEYE', 'DYNAMIC'
PAINTED BAKELITE, 5 TUBES, 1 BAND
WHITE $110, RED $175,
CHARTREUSE, BURGUNDY $125,
BLUE, BEIGE, GREEN, DK GREEN $140

CROSLEY 10-304 CA1950
'PLAYTIME'
STYRENE, 4 TUBES, 1 BAND
GRAY $100, MAROON $125, GREEN $125

CROSLEY 11-106 CA1053
'DECORATOR'
PAINTED BAKELITE, 5 TUBES, 1 BAND
BLACK, BEIGE $75
BURGUNDY, DK GREEN $90

CROSLEY 11-126 CA1953
PAINTED BAKELITE, 5 TUBES, 1 BAND
WHITE, BLACK $75
CHARTREUSE, MAROON $85
BLUE, GREEN $95

CROSLEY 11-113U CA1952
'JEWELERS'
GOLD REVERSE-PAINTED CLEAR STYRENE
5 TUBES, 1 BAND
$125

CROSLEY 11-114U CA1951
'SERENADER', 'LEFT BULLSEYE'
PAINTED BAKELITE, 5 TUBES, 1 BAND
IVORY, GREY $125, CHARTREUSE $150
BEIGE, BLUE-GREY $175, RED $200

CROSLEY 11-120U, D25 CA1951
'DASHBOARD'
PAINTED BAKELITE, 5 TUBES, 1 BAND
WHITE, BLACK, BLUE $125
CHARTREUSE, TAN, $175,
GREEN, MAROON $225

CROSLEY 11-301U CA1951
'RIVIERA'
PAINTED BAKELITE, 5 TUBES, 1 BAND
GREEN, BLUE, RED+TAN $125
BROWN+TAN $110, BLACK $125

CROSLEY 11AB, 52TG CA1941
BAKELITE, 5 TUBES, 1 BAND
BROWN OR PAINTED $45

CROSLEY 13AE, 52TD CA1941
BAKELITE, 5 TUBES, 2 BANDS
BROWN OR PAINTED $60
$50

CROSLEY 56PB CA1946
BAKELITE, 5 TUBES, 1 BAND
$75

CROSLEY 56TD CA1947
'DUETTE'
PAINTED BAKELITE, 5 TUBES, 1 BAND
IVORY+GOLD $175, MAROON+GOLD $225

CROSLEY 56TH CA1941
BAKELITE+ACRYLIC, 5 TUBES, 1 BAND
BROWN OR PAINTED $60

CROSLEY 62TA CA1942
BAKELITE, 6 TUBES, 2 BANDS
BROWN OR PAINTED $40

CROSLEY 66TA CA1946
BAKELITE, 6 TUBES, 2 BANDS
BROWN OR PAINTED $75

CROSLEY 519A, 529A CA1940
BAKELITE, 5 TUBES, 1 BAND
BROWN OR PAINTED $125

CROSLEY 519, 529 CA1939
BAKELITE, 5 TUBES, 1 BAND
BROWN OR PAINTED $110

CROSLEY 648A CA1940
BAKELITE, 5 TUBES, 1 BAND
BROWN OR PAINTED $125

CROSLEY 719 CA1939
BAKELITE, 7 TUBES, 2 BANDS
BROWN OR PAINTED $75

CROSLEY C548A CA1939
BAKELITE, 5 TUBES, 1 BAND
BROWN OR PAINTED $135

CROSLEY C588 'VANITY' CA1939
5 TUBES, 1 BAND
BAKELITE: BROWN OR PAINTED $125
IVORY PLASKON $225

CROSLEY E-10 CA1953
PAINTED BAKELITE, 5 TUBES, 1 BAND
WHITE $50, RED $75
BLUE, CHARTREUSE $65

CROSLEY E-15 CA1953
PAINTED BAKELITE, 5 TUBES, 1 BAND
DK BLUE, LT BLUE, CHARTREUSE $100
TAN $90, WHITE $75

CROSLEY G1465 CA1938
'SPLIT GRILLE'

CATALIN, 5 TUBES, 1 BAND
BLACK+YELLOW $5,000
MAROON+YELLOW $4,000
YELLOW+TORTOISE $3,500

CROSLEY E-75 CA1953
PAINTED BAKELITE, 5 TUBES, 1 BAND
WHITE, GRAY, TAN, BLACK $25
GREEN, CHARTREUSE $35, RED $45

CROSLEY JT3 'SUFFOLK' CA1955
PAINTED BAKELITE, 5 TUBES, 1 BAND
IVORY, BLACK $90
RED, GREEN $110

CRUSADER CA1941
BAKELITE, 5 TUBES, 1 BAND
BROWN OR PAINTED $50

DELCO 1134 CA1938
BAKELITE, 5 TUBES, 1 BAND
BROWN OR PAINTED $125

DELCO 1141 CA1946
BAKELITE, 6 TUBES, 1 BAND
BROWN OR PAINTED $175

DELCO 1244 CA1947
BAKELITE, 5 TUBES, 1 BAND
BROWN OR PAINTED $135

DELCO 1170 CA1942
BAKELITE, 5 TUBES, 1 BAND
BROWN OR PAINTED $65

DELCO 1230 CA1947
'RIBBON GRILLE'
BAKELITE, 5 TUBES, 1 BAND
BROWN OR PAINTED $75

CYARTS B CA1947

5 TUBES, 1 BAND
LUCITE+PLEXIGLASS
YELLOW $2500
RED $3500

DETROLA 199,219 CA1939
'SUPER PEE WEE'

5 TUBES, 1 BAND
BROWN BAKELITE $350
PLASKON: IVORY $450
GREEN+BEETLE $1800
LT BLUE+BEETLE $1500
RED+BEETLE $1500

DETROLA 218 CA1939
'PEE WEE'

4 TUBES, 1 BAND
BROWN BAKELUTE $275
IVORY PLASKON $450
RED PLASKON $1200
GREEN PLASKON $1400

DELCO R1234,6 CA1947
BAKELITE, 5 TUBES, 1 BAND
BROWN OR PAINTED $20

DELCO R1238 CA1948
STYRENE+BAKELITE, 5 TUBES, 1 BAND
$50

DETROLA 208, 283 CA1938
5 TUBES, 1 BAND
BAKELITE: BROWN $75
PLASKON: IVORY $200
RED $600, BEETLE $325

DETROLA 343 CA1941
'LARGE SPLIT GRILLE'
BAKELITE+TENITE, 5 TUBES, 1 BAND
$175

DETROLA CA1940
'PEE WEE CONVERTER'
BAKELITE, 3 TUBES, 1 BAND
$200

DEWALD 406 'BANTAM' CA1939
4 TUBES, 1 BAND
BROWN BAKELITE $275
IVORY PLASKON $425

DETROLA 274, 281 CA1939
'SPLIT GRILLE'
5 TUBES, 1 BAND
BEETLE+BLUE PLASKON $1700
BEETLE $ RED PLASKON $1700
BLUE+WHITE PLASKON $2500
MAROON +YELLOW CATALIN $4000
YELLOW +RED CATALIN $4000

DETROLA 272, 280 CA1939
'JUNIOR'
4 TUBES, 1 BAND
BROWN BAKELITE $150
IVORY PLASKON $250
RED PLASKON $750
GREEN PLASKON $750
BLUE PLASKON $750

DEWALD A501 CA1946
'HARP'
CATALIN, 5 TUBES,1 BAND
BROWN+YELLOW $750
RED+YELLOW $900
YELLOW $600

DEWALD 'BANTAM' CA1940
5 TUBES, 1 BAND
BROWN BAKELITE+IVORY $150
IVORY+RED PLASKON $250

DEWALD 538 CA1940
5 TUBES, 1 BAND
BROWN BAKELITE $125
PLASKON: IVORY $200, BEETLE $375

DEWALD 548,555 CA1939
5 TUBES, 1 BAND
BAKELITE: BLACK $400, BROWN $350
IVORY PLASKON $600

DEWALD B500 'LEADER' CA1948
BAKELITE, 5 TUBES, 1 BAND
BROWN OR PAINTED $20

DEWALD B504 CA1948
4 TUBES, 1 BAND, AC-DC
$125

DEWALD JD519 CA1946
STYRENE, 5 TUBES, 1 BAND
BROWN $60, IVORY $75, BLACK $75
MARBLED BROWN $125
MARBLED SALMON $175

DEWALD B403 CA1948
'HARP WITH CLOCK'
CATALIN, 5 TUBES, 1 BAND
YELLOW $600
MAROON $750
BROWN $650

DEWALD 561 CA1939
'JEWEL'
CATALIN, 5 TUBES, 1 BAND
YELLOW $800
YELLOW+BLUE $1500
YELLOW+MAROON $1200
MAROON+YELLOW $1200

DEWALD B512 CA1948
'JEWEL WITH CLOCK'
CATALIN, 5 TUBES, 1 BAND
ALABASTER $450
MAROON $500
BROWN $550

DEWALD C800 CA1949
BAKELITE, 5 TUBES, 1 BAND
BROWN OR PAINTED $25

DUNLOP CA1939
BAKELITE, 5 TUBES, 1 BAND
BROWN OR PAINTED $225

ECA 102 CA1947
BAKELITE, 5 TUBES, 1 BAND
BROWN OR PAINTED $35

ELECTRONIC CA1948
BAKELITE, 5 TUBES, 1 BAND
$50

ELECTRONIC CA1948
BAKELITE, 5 TUBES, 1 BAND
$50

ELECTROHOME 5T7 CA1956
STYRENE, 5 TUBES, 1 BAND
$25

ELECTROHOME 5T9 CA1956
STYRENE, 5 TUBES, 1 BAND
$20

ELECTROHOME 52-13A CA1952
STYRENE, 4 TUBES, 1 BAND
$20

ELECTROHOME 54-17R CA1954
STYRENE, 5 TUBES, 1 BAND
$30

ELECTROHOME 54-20 CA1954
STYRENE, 5 TUBES, 1 BAND
$15

ELECTROHOME 54-19 CA1954
STYRENE, 5 TUBES, 1 BAND
$20

ELECTROHOME P107 CA1953
STYRENE, 5 TUBES, 1 BAND
$15

ELECTROHOME PK104 CA1953
STYRENE, 5 TUBES, 1 BAND
$20

ELECTROHOME RM275 CA1956
STYRENE, 5 TUBES, 1 BAND
$20

ELECTROHOME RM276 CA1956
STYRENE, 5 TUBES, 1 BAND
$20

ELECTROHOME RM237 CA1956
STYRENE, 5 TUBES, 1 BAND
$20

ELECTROHOME 5C12 CA1956
STYRENE, 5 TUBES, 1 BAND
YELLOW $50, PINK $45

ELECTROHOME 5C12 CA1956
STYRENE, 5 TUBES, 1 BAND
YELLOW $50, PINK $45

EMERSON 17 'MIRACLE SIX' CA1935
4 TUBES, 1 BAND
BLACK BAKELITE+CHROME $900

EMERSON 19 CA1935
4 TUBES, 1 BAND
BROWN BAKELITE $250

EMERSON 20A CA1934
4 TUBES, 1 BAND
BROWN BAKELITE $450

EMERSON 126, 199 CA1937
5 TUBES, 1 BAND
BROWN BAKELITE $150

EMERSON 149 CA1937
5 TUBES, 2 BANDS
BROWN BAKELITE $50, IVORY PLASKON $125
IVORY PLASKON+BLACK BAKELITE $250

EMERSON 191 CA1938
5 TUBES, 1 BAND
BROWN BAKELITE $50
IVORY PLASKON $100

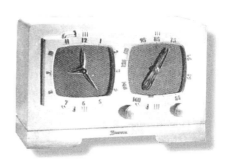

EMERSON 157 CA1937
'CLOCKETTE'
4 TUBES, 1 BAND
BROWN BAKELITE $110, IVORY PLASKON $200
IVORY PLASKON+BLACK BAKELITE $400

EMERSON 188 CA1938
4 TUBES, 1 BAND
BROWN BAKELITE $125, IVORY PLASKON $250
IVORY PLASKON+BLACK BAKELITE $600

EMERSON 198 'MYSTERY' CA1938
5 TUBES, 1 BAND
BROWN BAKELITE $90, IVORY PLASKON $175
IVORY PLASKON+BLACK BAKELITE $350

EMERSON 200 CA1938
5-6 TUBES, 2 BANDS
BROWN BAKELITE $50, IVORY PLASKON $175
IVORY PLASKON+BLACK BAKELITE $300

EMERSON 208 CA1938
5-6 TUBES, 2 BANDS
BROWN BAKELITE $50, IVORY PLASKON $175
IVORY PLASKON+BLACK BAKELITE $300

EMERSON 211 CA1938
(AX-211) 5 TUBES, 1 BAND
BROWN+BLACK BAKELITE $125
IVORY PLASKON+BLACK BAKELITE $350

EMERSON 108 CA1936
'U5A'

5 TUBES, 2 BANDS
BROWN BAKELITE $225
BLACK BAKELITE $300
IVORY PLASKON $450

EMERSON 190 CA1938
'AU190'

CATALIN, 5 TUBES, 2 BANDS
BLUE $4500
BROWN $2700
GREEN $2300
RED $3000
ALABASTER $1800

EMERSON 245 CA1938
'AU245'
'LOUVERED GRILLE'

CATALIN, 5 TUBES, 2 BANDS
BLUE+WHITE $5000
LT GREEN+WHITE $3500
RED+WHITE $5000
YELLOW+MAROON $2500
YELLOW+WHITE $1800

EMERSON 246 CA1938
'D-DIAL'
5 TUBES, 1 BAND
BROWN BAKELITE $150, IVORY PLASKON $325
PALE GREEN PLASKON $800

EMERSON 274 CA1939
5 TUBES, 2-3 BANDS
BROWN BAKELITE $100
IVORY PLASKON $200

EMERSON 255 CA1939
'PRE-WAR EMERSONETTE'
2 TUBES, 1 BAND
BROWN BAKELITE $175
BLACK BAKELITE $200
IVORY PLASKON $250
GREEN PLASKON$750
RED PLASKON $800

EMERSON 540 CA1947
'POST-WAR EMERSONETTE'
3 TUBES, 1 BAND
BROWN BAKELITE $125
BLACK BAKELITE $150
IVORY PLASKON $200
GREEN PLASKON$500
RED PLASKON $500

EMERSON 235 CA1938
'AX235'
'LITTLE MIRACLE'
CATALIN, 5 TUBES, 1 BAND
BLACK+ORANGE $4000
BLUE+WHITE $5000
GREEN+GREEN OR IVORY $3000
RED+IVORY $4000
YELLOW+BLACK $2000

EMERSON 258 CA1939
'BM258'
'BIG MIRACLE'
CATALIN, 5 TUBES, 1 BAND
BLUE $4500
GREEN $2500
MAROON $2500
YELLOW $1500

EMERSON 381 CA1941
5 TUBES, 1 BAND
BROWN BAKELITE $65
IVORY PLASKON $140
RED PLASKON $500
GREEN PLASKON $500

EMERSON 330 CA1941
5 TUBES, 1 BAND
BROWN BAKELITE $35
IVORY PLASKON $65

EMERSON 337 CA1941
6 TUBES, 2 BANDS
BROWN BAKELITE $35
IVORY PLASKON $75

EMERSON 336 C1940
5 TUBES, 1 BAND
BROWN BAKELITE $25
IVORY PLASKON $50

EMERSON 343 CA1940
ATTRIBUTED TO NORMAN BEL GEDDES
5 TUBES, 2 BANDS
BROWN BAKELITE $100
IVORY PLASKON $225

EMERSON 426 CA1942
BAKELITE, 4 TUBES, 1 BAND
$50

EMERSON 413, 441, 514 CA1947
BAKELITE, 5-6 TUBES, 1-2 BANDS
BROWN BAKELITE $45
IVORY PLASKON $90

EMERSON 375 CA1941
'FIVE PLUS ONE'
CATALIN, 5 TUBES, ONE BAND
ALABASTER+BROWN $2000
BLUE+TAN $4500
GREEN+ALABASTER $3500
RED+IVORY $4000

EMERSON 400, CA1940
'ARISTOCRAT'
NORMAN BEL GEDDES DESIGN
CATALIN, 5 TUBES, 1 BAND
BLACK+WHITE $2500
BROWN+WHITE $1200
DK GREEN+RED, WHITE $1800
LT GREEN+RED, WHITE $1800
YELLOW+BLACK, WHITE $1200
'PATRIOT'
BLUE+RED+WHITE $3800
WHITE+RED+BLUE $2000
RED+WHITE+BLUE $3000

EMERSON 520 CA1946
CATALIN, 5 TUBES, 1 BAND
BROWN+TAN MARBLE $250
BLACK+YELLOW MARBLE $375

EMERSON 575,656 C1952
STYRENE, 5 TUBES, 1 BAND AC-DC
BROWN $30, RED $75
GREEN $65, IVORY $50

EMERSON 421,515,1002 CA1946
6 TUBES, 2 BANDS
BROWN BAKELITE $25
IVORY PLASKON $60

EMERSON 509 CA1946
5 TUBES, 1 BAND
BROWN BAKELITE $20
IVORY PLASKON $35

EMERSON 547 CA1947
STYRENE, 5 TUBES, 1 BAND
BLACK $50, IVORY $75,
MARBLED GREEN $350, MARBLED TAN $225
TRANSPARENT BLUE, RED $750

EMERSON 578A CA1949
STYRENE, 5 TUBES, 1 BAND
BLACK $50,
IVORY, MAROON $75

EMERSON 561 CA1947
RAYMOND LOEWY ATTRIBUTED
5 TUBES, 1 BAND
BROWN BAKELITE $75, BLACK BAKELITE $100
IVORY PLASKON $150

EMERSON 517 CA1947
'MODERNE'

RAYMOND LOEWY DESIGN
5 TUBES, 1 BAND
BAKELITE: BROWN $50, BLACK $75
PLASKON: IVORY $135
IVORY+GOLD MARBLING $175
GREEN+GOLD MARBLING $500
RED+GOLD MARBLING $500

EMERSON 543 CA1947
5 TUBES, 1 BAND
BLACK BAKELITE $45
IVORY PLASKON $75

EMERSON 581 CA1950
5 TUBES, 1 BAND
BLACK BAKELITE $50
IVORY PLASKON $85

EMERSON 671 CA1951
5 TUBES, 1 BAND
BAKELITE: BROWN $30, BLACK $40
IVORY PLASKON $55

EMERSON 572 CA1949
'CLOCKETTE'
STYRENE, 5 TUBES, 1 BAND
BROWN $45, BLACK $75, IVORY 175,
MARBLED GREEN+WHITE $375
MARBLED BLACK+IVORY $350

EMERSON 602C CA1949
RAYMOND LOEWY ATTRIBUTED
STYRENE, 5 TUBES, 1 BAND
BROWN $40, BLACK $75,
IVORY $75, MAROON $100

EMERSON 610 CA1949
RAYMOND LOEWY ATTRIBUTED
STYRENE, 5 TUBES, 1 BAND
BROWN $40, BLACK $75,
IVORY $75, MAROON $100

EMERSON 646 CA1951
STYRENE, 4 TUBES, 1 BAND
BLACK OR IVORY $40
MAROON $65, ORANGE $90

EMERSON 652 CA1951
STYRENE, 5 TUBES, 1 BAND
BLACK OR IVORY $20

EMERSON 613 CA1949
'SHARK FIN'
STYRENE, 5 TUBES, 1 BAND
BLACK, IVORY $50
MAROON $65, GREEN $75

EMERSON 705,830,850 CA1952
STYRENE, 4 TUBES, 1 BAND
MAROON $60, GREY $50, GREEN $60
BLACK $70, PINK $100, YELLOW $125

EMERSON 706 CA1952
5 TUBES, 1 BAND
BROWN BAKELITE $40
PLASKON: IVORY $60, PINK $125
GREEN $150, RED $165

EMERSON 707 'SUNBURST' CA1953
5 TUBES, 1 BAND
BROWN BAKELITE $50
PLASKON: IVORY $70, PINK $150
GREEN $175, RED $175

EMERSON 724B CA1953
5 TUBES, 1 BAND
BAKELITE: BROWN $40, BLACK $60
PLASKON: IVORY $75, RED $175

EMERSON 808 CA1955
5 TUBES, 1 BAND
BLACK BAKELITE $60
PLASKON: IVORY $90, RED $200
DK RED $125, DK GREEN $135, GRAY $110

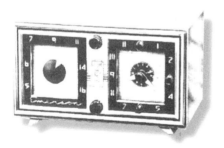

EMERSON 718 CA1954
STYRENE, 5 TUBES, 1 BAND
$25

EMERSON 729 CA1954
PLASKON+REVERSE-PAINTED GRILLE
IVORY $60, GREEN $100
BLUE $150, RED $175

EMERSON 744B CA1954
STYRENE, 5 TUBES, 1 BAND
NUMEROUS COLOR COMBINATIONS $750
NOTE: RARELY PERFECT - FRONT FEET TYPICALLY BROKEN OFF
AND NOT APPARENT UNLESS INSPECTED CLOSELY
VALUE IMPERFECTS AT 50%

EMERSON 778 CA1955
STYRENE, 5 TUBES, 1 BAND
BROWN, BLACK, IVORY $50
GREEN $125, RED $150

EMERSON 788,816 CA1955
STYRENE, 5 TUBES, 1 BAND
BROWN, BLACK, IVORY, GRAY $40
GREEN $75

EMERSON 790 CA1954
STYRENE, 5 TUBES, 1 BAND
BLACK $35, GREEN $75, GREY $50
MAROON $60, TAN $55

EMERSON 810B CA1955
STYRENE, 5 TUBES, 1 BAND, ILLUMINATED DIAL
BLACK, IVORY $90
MAROON $110

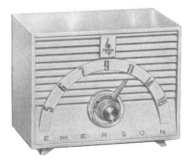

EMERSON 822 CA1955
STYRENE, 5 TUBES, 1 BAND
BROWN $25,
IVORY $30

EMERSON 812 CA1955
PLASKON, 5 TUBES, 1 BAND
BROWN $35, BLACK, IVORY $45
DK GREEN $90, GREY $60

EMERSON 813 CA1955
PLASKON, 5 TUBES, 1 BAND
BROWN $20, BLACK, IVORY $30
DK GREEN $60, GREY $40

EMERSON 823 CA1955
STYRENE, 5 TUBES, 1 BAND
BLACK, IVORY $75,
BROWN $50, GREEN $125, GREY $90

EMERSON 832 CA1956
STYRENE, 5 TUBES, 1 BAND
BROWN $20, BLACK, IVORY $30,
GREEN $60, GREY $40

EMERSON 825 CA1955
STYRENE, 5 TUBES, 1 BAND
BLACK, IVORY, GRAY $45
BROWN $35, GREEN $75

EMERSON 826 CA1955
STYRENE, 5 TUBES, 1 BAND
BLACK, IVORY, GRAY $60
BROWN $40, DK GREEN $75
LT GREEN, PINK $150, RED $225

EMERSON 846 CA1956
STYRENE, 5 TUBES, 1 BAND
BLACK, IVORY, GRAY, TAN $40
BROWN $25, GREEN $50
PINK $65, RED $125

EMERSON 876,881,917B CA1957
STYRENE, 5 TUBES, 1 BAND
BLACK, IVORY $30
TURQUOISE, PINK $60
GREEN $45

EMERSON 851 CA1956
STYRENE, 5 TUBES, 1 BAND
BLACK $60, IVORY $50
AQUA, PINK $90
GREEN $65

EMERSON 805B,833 CA1954
5 TUBES, 1 BAND, AC-DC
IVORY, GRAY, TAN $40
MAROON, GREEN $65

EMERSON 852 CA1956
STYRENE, 5 TUBES, 1 BAND
BLACK, IVORY $45
AQUA, PINK $110
GREEN $60

EMERSON 853 CA1956
STYRENE, 5 TUBES, 1 BAND
BLACK, IVORY $45
AQUA, PINK $110
GREEN $60

EMERSON 915 CA1958
STYRENE, 5 TUBES, 1 BAND
BLACK, IVORY $45
TURQUOISE $110
GREEN $60

EMERSON 1703 CA1961
STYRENE, 5 TUBES, 1 BAND
IVORY, TAN, GRAY $40
PINK, TURQUOISE $65

ESQUIRE 550U CA1956
STYRENE, 5 TUBES, 1 BAND
BROWN $35, IVORY $45

FADA 5F50, 740 CA1939
BAKELITE/PLASKON, 5 TUBES, 1 BAND
BROWN BAKELITE $75
IVORY PLASKON $165

FADA 6A51,L96 CA1939
5-6 TUBES, 1-2 BANDS
BROWN BAKELITE $110
IVORY PLASKON $175

FADA 44, 55 CA1940
5 TUBES, 1 BAND
BROWN BAKELITE $90
IVORY PLASKON $175

FADA 119, 790 CA1940
5 TUBES, 1 BAND - 8 TUBES, AM-FM
BROWN BAKELITE $75
IVORY PLASKON $150

FADA 200 CA1951
STYRENE, 5 TUBES, 1 BAND
BLACK, IVORY $75, BROWN $50
MAROON $90

FADA 209 CA1947
BAKELITE, 5 TUBES, 1 BAND
BROWN OR PAINTED $85

FADA 350 C1937
5 TUBES, 1 BAND
BROWN BAKELITE $200
IVORY PLASKON $350

FADA 550,855 CA1946
STYRENE, 5 TUBES, 1 BAND
IVORY MARBLE $200, BROWN MARBLE $175
MAROON $100

FADA 605,830 CA1950
STYRENE, 5 TUBES, 1 BAND
BROWN MARBLE $150
IVORY MARBLE $200

FADA 5F50 CA1939
'5F50'

CATALIN, 5 TUBES, 1 BAND
ALABASTER $2300
ALABASTER+GREEN $3500
ALABASTER+RED $3500
ALABASTER+TORTOISE $2800
ALABASTER+ONYX $2800
GREEN+ALABASTER $6000

FADA 5F60 CA1937
'5F60'

CATALIN, 5 TUBES, 1 BAND
ALABASTER $2000
ALABASTER+LT GREEN $3500
ALABASTER+RED $3500
ALABASTER+TORTOISE $2500
ALABASTER+ONYX $2500
GREEN+ALABASTER $5000

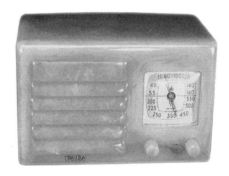

FADA 52 CA1938 L56
'52'

CATALIN, 5 TUBES, 1 BAND
ALABASTER $2500
ALABASTER+BLUE $4000
ALABASTER+RED $3500
ALABASTER+GREEN $3500
ALABASTER+TORTOISE $3500
ALABASTER+ONYX $3500
GREEN+ALABASTER $5000

FADA 115 CA1940
FADA 1000 C1946
'BULLET', 'STREAMLINER'
CATALIN, 5 TUBES, 1 BAND
ALABASTER $1300
ALABASTER+RED $2000
BLUE+ALABASTER $5000
MAROON+ALABASTER $1800
ONYX+ALABASTER $3500
GREEN+ALABASTER $4500

FADA 252,353,659 CA1941
'TEMPLE'
5 TUBES, 1 BAND
ALABASTER $1200
ALABASTER+RED $1700
BLUE+ALABASTER $5000
MAROON+ALABASTER $1700
ONYX+ALABASTER $2800

FADA 700 CA1947
'CLOUD'
CATALIN, 5 TUBES, 1 BAND
ALABASTER+BROWN $1500
ALABASTER+RED $1500
ALABASTER+WHITE $1300
BLUE+WHITE $5000
MAROON+WHITE $1800
ONYX+WHITE $2700

FADA 845 CA1950
'CLOUD'
STYRENE, 5 TUBES, 1 BAND
BROWN $350
IVORY $425
MAROON $375

FADA 242,246,250 SERIES CA1936
'STREAMLINER'
5-6 TUBES, 2 BANDS
BROWN BAKELITE $125
BLACK BAKELITE+GOLD TRIM $500
BLACK BAKELITE+CHROME TRIM $500
IVORY PLASKON $375
IVORY PLASKON+GOLD TRIM $750
RED PLASKON $1700
RED PLASKON+GOLD TRIM $2000

FADA 254, 260 CA1937
'SWASTIKA'
254 SERIES-3 KNOBS, 260 SERIES-2 KNOBS
5 TUBES, 1 BAND
BROWN BAKELITE $225
BLACK BAKELITE $300
BLACK BAKELITE+CHROME TRIM $650
IVORY PLASKON $375
IVORY PLASKON+GOLD TRIM $750
RED PLASKON $1500
RED PLASKON+GOLD TRIM $2000

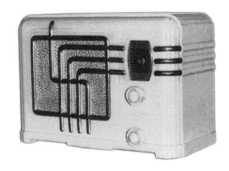

FADA 454,460 CA1938
'DOUBLE-Z'
454 SERIES-3 KNOBS, 460 SERIES-2 KNOBS
5 TUBES, 1 BAND
BROWN BAKELITE $175
BLACK BAKELITE $250
BLACK BAKELITE+CHROME TRIM $550
IVORY PLASKON $350
IVORY PLASKON+GOLD TRIM $600
RED PLASKON $1500
RED PLASKON+GOLD TRIM $2000

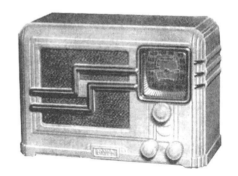

FADA 777 CA1947
6 TUBES, 2 BANDS
BROWN BAKELITE $80
IVORY PLASKON $125

FADA L56A CA1939
BAKELITE, 5 TUBES, 1 BAND
BROWN OR PAINTED $225

FADA 'SILENTRADIO' CA1940
5 TUBES, 1 BAND
BROWN BAKELITE $125
IVORY PLASKON $225

FADA P80 CA1947
4 TUBES, 1 BAND, DC
BAKELITE: BLACK, MAROON $225
IVORY PLASKON $250

FADA P111 CA1949
BAKELITE, 4 TUBES, 1 BAND, DC
BROWN $60
BLACK, MAROON $90

FARNSWORTH BT50 CA1941
BAKELITE, 5 TUBES, 1 BAND
BROWN OR PAINTED $20

FADA 1005 CA1947

STYRENE, 5 TUBES, 1 BAND
BROWN $175
IVORY $200
MAROON $250
COBALT BLUE $500

FADA 711 CA1947

CATALIN+STYRENE
5 TUBES, 1 BAND
ALABASTER $1200
BLUE $3500
GREEN $2500
RED$1700

FEDERAL CA1938 'SPECIAL'

6 TUBES, 2 BANDS
CATALIN CABINET, PLASKON FACE
BLACK+LAVENDER $7500
BLACK+BLUE $6000
BLACK+RED $6000

FARNSWORTH AT10 CA1939
5 TUBES, 1 BAND
BROWN BAKELITE $125
PLASKON: IVORY $250, BEETLE $450

FARNSWORTH AT-14 CA1940
5 TUBES, 1 BAND
BROWN BAKELITE $175
PLASKON: IVORY $300, BEETLE $500

FARNSWORTH BT52,3 CA1941
5 TUBES, 1 BAND
BROWN BAKELITE $50
PLASKON: IVORY $150, BEETLE $300

FARNSWORTH AT21 CA1940
5 TUBES, 1 BAND
BROWN BAKELITE $90
PLASKON: IVORY $175, BEETLE $400

FARNSWORTH CT50 CA1942
BAKELITE, 5-6 TUBES, 1 BAND
BROWN OR PAINTED $15

FARNSWORTH CT61,ET51 CA1946
BAKELITE+METAL, 6 TUBES, 1 BAND
BLACK $75
BROWN OR PAINTED $50

**FARNSWORTH GT-50 CA1948
'BULLET'**
BAKELITE, 5 TUBES, 1 BAND
BROWN OR PAINTED $150
BLACK $175

FARNSWORTH GT60 CA1948
6 TUBES, 2 BANDS
BROWN BAKELITE+MARBLED TAN GRILLE
$75

FARNSWORTH CT43 CA1942
BAKELITE, 5 TUBES, 1 BAND
$25

FEDERAL 1040 CA1947
5 TUBES, 1 BAND
PLASKON: IVORY $110, IVORY+GOLD $125
BAKELITE: BROWN $40, BLACK $60,
BLACK+GOLD $75
PAINTED: AQUA & GOLD $90

FEDERAL 1024,1029 CA1947
BAKELITE, 5 TUBES, 1 BAND
BROWN OR PAINTED $20

FIRESTONE 4-A-11 CA1950
BAKELITE, 5 TUBES, 1 BAND
BROWN OR PAINTED $50
BLACK $65

FIRESTONE 4-A-12 CA1949
BAKELITE, 5 TUBES, 1 BAND
BROWN OR PAINTED $110

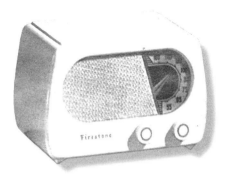

FIRESTONE 4-A-78 CA1950
BAKELITE, 5 TUBES, 1 BAND
BROWN OR PAINTED $40
IVORY $45

FIRESTONE 4-A-108 CA1954
BAKELITE, 5 TUBES, 1 BAND
BROWN OR PAINTED $35

FIRESTONE 4-A-101 CA1954
BAKELITE, 5 TUBES, 1 BAND
BROWN OR PAINTED $30

FIRESTONE 4-A-121 CA1954
BAKELITE, 5 TUBES, 1 BAND
BROWN OR PAINTED $20

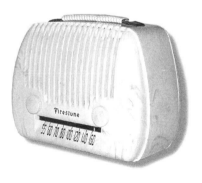

FIRESTONE 4-C-17 CA1954
STYRENE, 4 TUBES, 1 BAND
MARBLED BROWN $60
IVORY $50, MARBLED IVORY $110

FIRESTONE S-7402-1 CA1939
5 TUBES, 1 BAND
BROWN BAKELITE $75
PLASKON: IVORY $135, BEETLE $250

FIRESTONE S-7402-5 CA1941
BAKELITE, 5 TUBES, 1 BAND
BROWN OR PAINTED $35
BLACK $50

FIRESTONE S-7402-7 CA1941
BAKELITE, 5 TUBES, 1 BAND
BROWN OR PAINTED $35
BLACK $50

FIRESTONE S-7403-2 CA1941
BAKELITE, 5 TUBES, 1 BAND
BROWN OR PAINTED $40
BLACK $60

FIRESTONE S-7425-6 CA1939
'WORLD'S FAIR'
BAKELITE, 5 TUBES, 1 BAND
BROWN OR PAINTED $300, BLACK $375
IVORY PLASKON $550

FIRESTONE S-7427-5 CA1939
BAKELITE, 4 TUBES, 1 BAND
BROWN OR PAINTED $60
BLACK $75
IVORY PLASKON $135

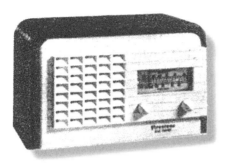

FIRESTONE S-7428-1 CA1939
4 TUBES, 1 BAND, DC
BROWN BAKELITE+IVORY PLASKON $50
BLACK BAKELITE+IVORY PLASKON $75

FUTURAMIST CA1960
STYRENE, 4 TUBES, 1 BAND
BLACK, IVORY, GRAY $40
AQUA, PINK $75

**GAROD 5A1,D1443 CA1941
'ENSIGN'**
5 TUBES, 1 BAND
BROWN OR PAINTED BAKELITE $75
IVORY PLASKON $175

GAROD 5A2 CA1946
PAINTED BAKELITE, 5 TUBES, 1 BAND
IVORY WITH BLUE OR RED GRILLE $100
GREEN GRILLE $115

GAROD 6B1 'SENATOR' CA1941
5 TUBES, 1 BAND
BROWN OR PAINTED BAKELITE $50
IVORY PLASKON $125

GAROD XA-49 CA1949
5 TUBES, 1 BAND
BROWN OR PAINTED BAKELITE $75
BLACK BAKELITE $125

GAROD 6-AU1 CA1940
'COMMANDER'
CATALIN, 5 TUBES, 1 BAND
MAROON+YELLOW $2000,
RED+YELLOW $2500
YELLOW+RED $2000
YELLOW $1200

1B-55L
YELLOW $1200
CARAMEL+TORTOISE $4000
DK GREEN+LT GREEN $7000
MAROON+YELLOW 2000

NOTES: 6AU1 GRILLE WRAPS AROUND LEFT SIDE
1B-55L GRILL IS FLUSH TO FRONT - NO WRAP
DEDUCT 20% VALUE FOR VISIBLE GRILL SCREWS

GAROD 256 CA1941
'PEAK-TOP'
CATALIN, 5 TUBES, 1 BAND
IVORY $1700
IVORY+BLUE $4000
IVORY+RED $2800
MAROON+IVORY $2800

GE 50 CA1948
BAKELITE, 5 TUBES, 1 BAND
BROWN OR PAINTED $30

GE 60,65 CA1948
BAKELITE, 5 TUBES, 1 BAND
BROWN OR PAINTED $25

GE 123,401,415 CA1952
STYRENE, 5 TUBES, 1 BAND
BROWN, WHITE $20
BROWN MARBLED $40

GE 136,422 CA1950
STYRENE, 5 TUBES, 1 BAND
BROWN, WHITE $25
BROWN MARBLED $50

GE 202 CA1947
5 TUBES, 1 BAND
BROWN BAKELITE $40
IVORY PLASKON $60

GE 220 CA1947
5 TUBES, 1 BAND
BROWN BAKELITE $40
IVORY PLASKON $60

GE 210 CA1948
BAKELITE, 5 TUBES, 1 BAND
BROWN OR PAINTED $20

GE 218 CA1950
BAKELITE, 8 TUBES, AM-FM
BROWN OR PAINTED $25

GE 226 CA1950
BAKELITE, 5 TUBES, 1 BAND
BROWN OR PAINTED $15

GE 356 CA1948
BAKELITE, 5 TUBES, 1 BAND
BROWN OR PAINTED $20

GE 370 CA1949
BAKELITE, 8 TUBES, AM-FM
BROWN OR PAINTED $80
BLACK $125

GE 409,440 CA1954
'ATOMIC'
BROWN STYRENE, 8 TUBES, AM-FM
$85

GE 419 CA1954
STYRENE, 5 TUBES, 1 BAND
BROWN, BLACK, IVORY $15
GREEN $35, RED $60

GE 424,638 CA1955
STYRENE, 6 TUBES, 1 BAND
BROWN, BLACK, IVORY $35
GREEN $60, RED $125

GE 436 CA1954
STYRENE, 8 TUBES, AM-FM
BROWN MARBLE $50

GE 427 CA1954
STYRENE, 5 TUBES, 1 BAND
BLACK, WHITE $45
GREEN $60, PINK $75, RED $110

GE 475,621 CA1955
STYRENE, 6 TUBES, 1 BAND
BROWN, GRAY $25
LT BLUE $60

**GE 672, 673,
674 CA1955**
STYRENE, 6 TUBES, 1 BAND
BROWN, IVORY $20
RED $60

GE 555 CA1954
STYRENE, 5 TUBES, 1 BAND
BROWN, BLACK, IVORY $15
RED $45

GE 560 CA1954
STYRENE, 5 TUBES, 1 BAND
TAN, BLACK, IVORY $25
PINK, AQUA $65

GE 564 CA1954
STYRENE, 5 TUBES, 1 BAND
GRAY, BLACK, IVORY $20
PINK $65, GREEN $45

GE 606 CA1951
STYRENE, 4 TUBES, 1 BAND
BLACK, GRAY $30
MAROON, GREEN $40

GE 612 CA1954
STYRENE, 4 TUBES, 1 BAND
BLACK $100
GREEN $125, RED $175

GE 860 'ATOMIC' CA1954
STYRENE, 5 TUBES, 1 BAND
BLACK, GRAY, TAN $50
PINK, LT BLUE $100, RED $135

GE 913, C430 CA1960
STYRENE, 5 TUBES, 1 BAND
IVORY, TAN $35
PINK $60

GE 920 CA1957
STYRENE, 5 TUBES, 1 BAND
BROWN, GRAY $25
LT BLUE $50

GE C405 CA1960
STYRENE, 5 TUBES, 1 BAND
GREY $30, PINK $55

GE C421 CA1960
STYRENE, 6 TUBES, 1 BAND
BLUE $70, PINK $80

GE C435 CA1960
5 TUBES, 1 BAND
WHITE $20

GE C440 CA1960
5 TUBES, 1 BAND
BLUE $50, BLACK $20

GE F51 CA1937
5 TUBES, 1 BAND
BROWN BAKELITE $125
IVORY PLASKON $200

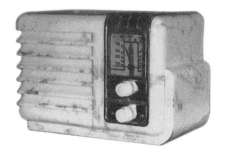

GE GD520 CA1939
PLASKON, 5 TUBES, 1 BAND
BEETLE $350

GE H400 CA1939
4 TUBES, 1 BAND
BROWN BAKELITE $125
PLASKON: IVORY $175, LT BLUE $450,
RED $600, BEETLE $350

GE H406U C.1939
'BANTAM'
4 TUBES, 1 BAND
BROWN BAKELITE $250

GE H500 CA1939
5 TUBES, 1 BAND
BROWN BAKELITE $125
PLASKON: IVORY $200, BEETLE $350

H510 CA1939
5 TUBES, 1 BAND
BROWN BAKELITE $150
PLASKON: IVORY $225, BEETLE $375

GE H600,J644 CA1939
6 TUBES, 1 BAND
BROWN BAKELITE $45
PLASKON: IVORY $75, BEETLE $135

GE J54,L500 CA 1941
5 TUBES, 1 BAND
BROWN BAKELITE $20
PLASKON: IVORY $50, BEETLE $110

GE J600, L600 CA1942
BAKELITE, 6 TUBES, 1 BAND
BROWN OR PAINTED $20

GE J614, J664 CA1941
BAKELITE, 6 TUBES, 1 BAND
BROWN OR PAINTED $20

GE JB420 CA9141
BAKELITE, 5 TUBES, 1 BAND
BROWN OR PAINTED $25

GE F40, L40 C.1937
4 TUBES, 1 BAND
BROWN OR PAINTED BAKELITE $150
IVORY PLASKON $225

GE L-650 CA1942
5 TUBES, 1 BAND
BROWN BAKELITE $45
IVORY PLASKON $80

GE T16A CA1956
STYRENE, 5 TUBES, 1 BAND
GRAY, TAN $20
PINK, BLUE $35

GE X105 CA1942
BAKELITE, 5 TUBES, 3 BANDS
BROWN OR PAINTED $25

GE L-512 CA1941
6 TUBES, 2 BANDS
BROWN BAKELITE+YELLOW CATALIN TRIM
$150

GE L570 CA1941
CATALIN, 5 TUBES, 1 BAND
YELLOW $750
BLACK+YELLOW $2500
MAROON+YELLOW $1800
YELLOW+MAROON $1500

GE T145 CA1960
STYRENE, TRANSISTORIZED, 1 BAND
GREY $45, BROWN $35

GE T120 CA1960
STYRENE, 9 TUBES, AM-FM
TAN $30

CGE C48B,C122 CA1949
5 TUBES, 1 BAND
BROWN BAKELITE $20
PLASKON: IVORY $50, BEETLE $110

CGE C401 CA1952
BAKELITE, 4 TUBES, 1 BAND
BROWN BAKELITE $60
IVORY PLASKON $110

CGE C402,404C404 CA1952
5 TUBES, 1 BAND
BROWN BAKELITE $30
IVORY PLASKON $65

CGE C400 CA1940
4 TUBES, 1 BAND
BROWN BAKELITE $110
IVORY PLASKON $150
PALE BLUE SPECKLED PLASKON $400

CGE 5 TUBES, 1 BAND
BROWN BAKELITE $40
IVORY PLASKON $80

CGE H52,JK52,KL52 CA1940
5 TUBES, 1 BAND
BROWN BAKELITE $90
IVORY PLASKON $175

GENERAL TELEVISION 5BY5 CA1940
5 TUBES, 1 BAND
BROWN BAKELITE $40
IVORY PLASKON $90

GENERAL TELEVISION 9A5 CA1948
BAKELITE, 5 TUBES, 1 BAND
BROWN+IVORY $75
BLACK+IVORY $100

GENERAL TELEVISION 588 CA1940
'TORPEDO'
5 TUBES, 1 BAND
BROWN OR PAINTED $175
IVORY PLASKON $300

GENERAL TELEVISION 'A' CA1947
5 TUBES, 1 BAND
BAKELITE: BROWN $125, BLACK $150
GREEN MARBLE TENITE $500

GENERAL TELEVISION 696 CA1940
6 TUBES, 2 BANDS
BROWN BAKELITE $175
IVORY PLASKON $325

GENERAL TELEVISION CA1940
'PEEWEE'
4 TUBES, 1 BAND
BROWN OR PAINTED BAKELITE $150
IVORY PLASKON $250

**GENERAL TELEVISION CA 1939
'TELETONE'**
6 TUBES, 1 BAND
BROWN BAKELITE $150
IVORY PLASKON $250

**GENERAL TELEVISION CA 1939
'TELETONE PUSHBUTTON'**
6 TUBES, 1 BAND
BROWN BAKELITE $175
IVORY PLASKON $300

GILFILLAN CA1938
5 TUBES, 1 BAND
BROWN OR PAINTED BAKELITE $40
IVORY PLASKON $75

GILFILLAN 5F CA1942
5 TUBES, 1 BAND
BROWN OR PAINTED BAKELITE $50
IVORY PLASKON $85

GILFILLAN 58M CA1947
BAKELITE, 5 TUBES, 1 BAND
BROWN OR PAINTED $150
BLACK $175

GILFILLAN 15F CA1942
BAKELITE, 5 TUBES, 1 BAND
BROWN OR PAINTED $75

GLOBETROTTER 3940 CA1939
4-5 TUBES, 1 BAND
BAKELITE: BROWN $75, BLACK $100
PLASKON: RED $450, IVORY $125

GLOBETROTTER 3952 CA1939
5 TUBES, 1 BAND
BROWN BAKELITE $50
IVORY PLASKON $75

GLOBETROTTER 3954 CA1939
5 TUBES, 1 BAND
BAKELITE: BROWN $150, BLACK $175
IVORY PLASKON $250

GOLDENTONE A1 CA1940
BAKELITE, 5 TUBES, 1 BAND
BROWN OR PAINTED $75

GOLDENTONE G1 CA1940
4 TUBES, 1 BAND
BROWN BAKELITE $100
IVORY PLASKON $175

GOLDENTONE 1A3 CA1942
BAKELITE, 5 TUBES, 1 BAND
BROWN OR PAINTED $75

GOLDENTONE 1A1 CA1940
6 TUBES, 2 BANDS
BROWN BAKELITE $50
IVORY PLASKON $90

GOLDENTONE 2A1 CA1940
6 TUBES, 2 BANDS
BROWN BAKELITE $65
IVORY PLASKON $125

GOLDENTONE 1C1,1C2 CA1940
5 TUBES, 1 BAND
BROWN BAKELITE $75
BEETLE PLASKON $300

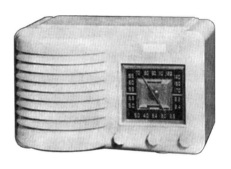

GOLDENTONE 1G1 CA1940
6 TUBES, 2 BANDS
BROWN BAKELITE $175
IVORY PLASKON $300

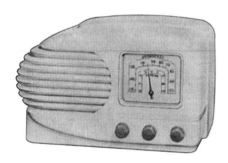

GOLDENTONE 1W3 CA1940
BAKELITE, 6 TUBES, 2 BANDS
BROWN OR PAINTED $150

GOLDENTONE 2W1 CA1940
5 TUBES, 1 BAND
BROWN OR PAINTED $175

GOLDENTONE 1W5 CA1940
5 TUBES, 1 BAND
BROWN OR PAINTED $35

GOLDENTONE 1W11 CA1942
5 TUBES, 1 BAND
BROWN OR PAINTED $45

GOLDENTONE 1W13 CA1942
5 TUBES, 1 BAND
BROWN OR PAINTED $50

GOLDENTONE 1W15 CA1942
6 TUBES, 2 BANDS
BROWN OR PAINTED $25

GOLDENTONE 2S1 CA1940
5 TUBES, 1 BAND
BROWN OR PAINTED $250

GOLDENTONE 6W12 CA1942
5 TUBES, 1 BAND
BROWN OR PAINTED $15

GOLDENTONE 199B CA1939
5 TUBES, 1 BAND
BROWN BAKELITE $225
IVORY PLASKON $350

GOLDENTONE 272 CA1939
4 TUBES, 1 BANDS
BROWN BAKELITE $100
IVORY PLASKON $175

GOLDENTONE 'BAINE' CA1939
BAKELITE, 5 TUBES, 1 BAND
BROWN OR PAINTED $125
BLACK $150

GOLDENTONE IC12 CA1942
BAKELITE, 5 TUBES, 1 BAND
BROWN OR PAINTED $25

GRANTLINE 58A CA1947
BAKELITE, 5 TUBES, 1 BAND
BROWN OR PAINTED $110
BLACK $135

GRANCO CR CA1959
STYRENE, 8 TUBES, AM-FM
WHITE $20
GRAY $30

GREBE CA1937
'CHALLENGER 1,2,5'

5 TUBES, 1 BAND
BROWN BAKELITE $150
BLACK BAKELITE $175
IVORY PLASKON $275
RED PLASKON $750
GREEN PLASKON $750

GREBE CA1937
'CHALLENGER 3'

5 TUBES, 1 BAND
BROWN BAKELITE $175
BLACK BAKELITE $225
IVORY PLASKON $325
RED PLASKON $850
GREEN PLASKON $850

HALSON CA1939
'DWARF'

CATALIN, 5 TUBES, 1 BAND
ALABASTER $6,500
GREEN $8,000
RED $10,000

GRANCO FM CA1959
STYRENE, 8 TUBES, AM-FM, DC
GREY $35, AQUA $70, PINK $70
MAROON $50

GRANCO T-160 CA1956
STYRENE, 8 TUBES, FM ONLY
BLACK $25, WHITE $20

GRANCO 730 CA1956
STYRENE, 8 TUBES, AM-FM
BLACK $25

HALLICRAFTERS EC102 CA1946
BAKELITE, 6 TUBES, 2 BANDS
BROWN OR PAINTED $45

HALLICRAFTERS S80 CA1952
BAKELITE, 5 TUBES, 1 BAND
BROWN OR PAINTED $15

**HALLICRAFTERS CANADA
ATCL11 CA1954**
5 TUBES, 1 BANDS
BROWN OR PAINTED $35

HALLICRAFTERS ATX13 CA1954
STYRENE, 5 TUBES, 1 BAND
IVORY, TAN $50
GREEN $65

HALLICRAFTERS 612 CA1954
STYRENE, 5 TUBES, 1 BAND
DK GREEN+LT GREEN $125
TAN+BROWN $75

IMPERIAL 104N CA1941
BAKELITE, 4 TUBES, 1 BAND
BROWN OR PAINTED $30

IMPERIAL 576-5Q CA1941
5 TUBES, 1 BAND
1208 $125

IMPERIAL 1501N CA1941
BAKELITE, 5 TUBES, 1 BAND
BROWN OR PAINTED $125

JEWEL 300 CA1940
STYRENE, 4 TUBES, 1 BAND
IVORY+GRAY MARBELED $125
IVORY+RED MARBELED $150

JEWEL 89,402 CA1951
'WAKEMASTER'
STYRENE, 5 TUBES, 1 BAND
BLACK+IVORY $40
IVORY $25

JEWEL 181A,700 CA1951
'ALWAYS'
STYRENE, 4 TUBES, 1 BAND
$40

JEWEL 98 CA1951
'WAKEMASTER'
STYRENE, 5 TUBES, 1 BAND
BROWN $20, IVORY $30

JEWEL 400 CA1951
STYRENE, 4 TUBES, 1 BAND
BROWN $45, IVORY $70

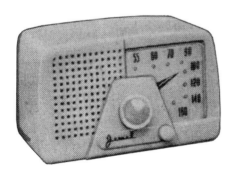

JEWEL 956 CA1950
STYRENE, 5 TUBES, 1 BAND
BROWN $25, IVORY $40

JEWEL 181 CA1951
STYRENE, 5 TUBES, 1 BAND
BROWN $25, IVORY $40

JEWEL 5100S CA1954
STYRENE, 4 TUBES, 1 BAND
BROWN $20, IVORY $30

KNIGHT 5H605 CA1951
STYRENE, 5 TUBES, 1 BAND
BROWN $30, IVORY $40

KADETTE "F" CA1932
'JUNIOR'
2 TUBES, 1 BAND
BROWN BAKELITE $250
BROWN SPECKLE MARBLE $350
BROWN BLOTCH MARBLE $425
RED PLASKON $750

KADETTE K-150 C.1938
'CAMEO'
BAKELITE, 5 TUBES, 1 BAND
BROWN $350
BROWN MARBLED $450

KADETTE 'KADETTE' CA1932
4 TUBES, 1 BAND
BROWN BAKELITE $275, IVORY PLASKON $400
BEETLE $750*

KADETTE L-25,29 'TOPPER' CA1937
5 TUBES, 1 BAND
L25-IVORY PLASKON+BLACK BAKELITE $750*
L29-WOOD $500*

KNIGHT 5F-565 CA1951
STYRENE
1256 $40

KNIGHT 5H678,679 CA1951
STYRENE, 5 TUBES, 1 BAND, CLOCK/RADIO
5H678-BROWN $35
5H679-IVORY $50

KNIGHT 6H590,591 CA1951
STYRENE, 6 TUBES, 1 BAND
6H590-BROWN $35
6H591-IVORY $45

KNIGHT 8G200,201 CA1951
BAKELITE, 8 TUBES, AM-FM
8G200-BROWN $110
8G201-IVORY $125

KADETTE K-10 'CLASSIC' CA1936
5 TUBES, 2 BANDS
PLASKON+TENITE+ACRYLIC
7 COLOR COMBINATIONS $1500

NOTE: RARELY FOUND NEAR PERFECT

KADETTE K25 CA1938
'CLOCKETTE'
CATALIN, 6 TUBES, 1 BAND
ALABASTER $2500
RED $7500, GREEN $4500
BLUE $7500
TRANSPARENT BLUE $8000

KADETTE 40 CA1935
'JEWEL'
4 TUBES, 1 BAND
BROWN BAKELITE $350
BLACK BAKELITE $400
IVORY PLASKON $450
RED PLASKON $750
BROWN BLOTCHED 'PEANUT BUTTER' $650
LAVENDER MARBLE $1200

KNIGHT 101 CA1942
5 TUBES, 1 BAND
BROWN OR PAINTED BAKELITE $65
IVORY PLASKON $120

KNIGHT 108 CA1942
BAKELITE, 6 TUBES, 2 BANDS
BROWN OR PAINTED BAKELITE $75
IVORY PLASKON $125

KNIGHT 10801 CA1939
'PEE WEE'
4 TUBES, 1 BAND
BROWN OR PAINTED BAKELITE $90
IVORY PLASKON $150

KNIGHT 10840 CA1939
5 TUBES, 1 BAND
BROWN OR PAINTED BAKELITE $150
IVORY PLASKON $250

KNIGHT 10830 CA1940
5 TUBES, 1 BAND
BROWN OR PAINTED BAKELITE $75
IVORY PLASKON $125

KNIGHT 10845 CA1939
5 TUBES, 1 BAND
BROWN OR PAINTED BAKELITE $90
IVORY PLASKON $135

KNIGHT 17126 CA1941
BAKELITE, 5 TUBES, 1 BAND
BROWN OR PAINTED

KNIGHT 17127 CA1941
CATALIN, 5 TUBES, 1 BAND
ALABASTER+GREEN $1800
ALABASTER+GREEN $1500

KNIGHT A9701 CA1937
5 TUBES, 1 BAND
BAKELITE: BLACK $100, BROWN $65
PLASKON: IVORY $140, RED $750

KNIGHT B10502 CA1938
5 TUBES, 2 BANDS
BAKELITE: BLACK $110, BROWN $75
PLASKON: IVORY $150, BEETLE $300, RED $750

KNIGHT 10860 CA1939
5 TUBES, 1 BAND
BROWN OR PAINTED BAKELITE $45
IVORY PLASKON $95

KNIGHT B10531 CA1941
5 TUBES, 2 BANDS
BROWN OR PAINTED BAKELITE $50

KNIGHT B10507 CA1941
5 TUBES, 1 BAND
BROWN OR PAINTED BAKELITE $75
IVORY PLASKON $135

KNIGHT B10509 CA1941
'TINY KNIGHT'
4 TUBES, 1 BAND
BROWN OR PAINTED BAKELITE $65
IVORY PLASKON $110

KNIGHT B10530,10531 CA1938
CHROME TRIM, 5 TUBES, 1 BAND
BLACK BAKELITE $225
IVORY PLASKON $300

LAFAYETTE 1-427 CA1953
STYRENE, 4 TUBES, 1 BAND
IVORY $30, BROWN $25
BROWN+TAN $45, MAROON+IVORY $60

KNIGHT B10536 CA1941
BAKELITE, 5 TUBES, 2 BANDS
BROWN OR PAINTED $40
BLACK $75

KNIGHT B10555 CA1941
5 TUBES, 2 BANDS
BROWN OR PAINTED BAKELITE $75
IVORY PLASKON $150, BEETLE PLASKON $250

KNIGHT Y737 CA1959
STYRENE, 5 TUBES, 1 BAND
$25

LAFAYETTE 1-573 CA1953
STYRENE, 5 TUBES, 1 BAND
$20

LAFAYETTE 1N-435 CA1950
STYRENE, 4 TUBES, 1 BAND
BROWN $45, IVORY $70

LAFAYETTE 1N-551 CA1950
'RANGER'
STYRENE, 5 TUBE, 1 BAND
BROWN $35, IVORY $45

LAFAYETTE 1N-562 CA1950
STYRENE, 5 TUBES, 1 BAND
BROWN $30, IVORY $50

LAFAYETTE 1N-819 CA1950
BAKELITE, 8 TUBE, AM-FM
BROWN OR PAINTED $15

LAFAYETTE 1R-413 CA1948
BAKELITE, 5 TUBES, 1 BAND
$50

LAFAYETTE 1R-521 CA1948
5 TUBES, 1 BAND
BROWN BAKELITE $35
IVORY PLASKON $65

LAFAYETTE 1R-708 CA1948
BAKELITE, 7 TUBES, FM
$50

LAFAYETTE 1R-805 CA1948
BAKELITE, 8 TUBES, FM
$65

LAFAYETTE 115K CA1953
BAKELITE, 5 TUBES, 1 BAND
BROWN OR PAINTED $30

LAFAYETTE 812K CA1953
BAKELITE, 5 TUBES, 2 BANDS
BROWN OR PAINTED $15

LAFAYETTE B-49 CA1939
5 TUBES, 1 BAND
BROWN OR PAINTED BAKELITE $75
IVORY PLASKON $125

LAFAYETTE BB-22 C.1940
BAKELITE, 5 TUBES, 1 BAND
BROWN OR PAINTED BAKELITE $350
IVORY PLASKON $500

LAFAYETTE BE-78 CA1939
BAKELITE, 5 TUBES, 1 BAND
BROWN OR PAINTED $350

LAFAYETTE CC-92 CA1939
BAKELITE, 5 TUBES, 1 BAND
BROWN OR PAINTED $75

LAFAYETTE D-24 CA1939
5 TUBES, 1 BAND
BROWN OR PAINTED BAKELITE $100
IVORY PLASKON $165

LAFAYETTE D-43 CA1939
5 TUBES, 1 BAND
BROWN OR PAINTED BAKELITE $175
IVORY PLASKON $325

LAFAYETTE D-58 CA1939
BAKELITE, 6 TUBES, 1 BAND
BROWN OR PAINTED $175

LAFAYETTE EM-70 CA1938
5 TUBES, 1 BAND
BROWN OR PAINTED BAKELITE $175
IVORY PLASKON $275

LAFAYETTE D-72 CA1939
BAKELITE, 6 TUBES, 2 BANDS
BROWN OR PAINTED $150

LAFAYETTE D-247 CA1942
BAKELITE, 5 TUBES, 1 BAND
BROWN OR PAINTED $60

LAFAYETTE E-22 CA1940
BAKELITE, 5 TUBES, 2 BANDS
BROWN OR PAINTED $75

LAFAYETTE E-38 CA1940
BAKELITE, 5 TUBES, 1 BAND
BROWN OR PAINTED $50

LAFAYETTE C3 CA1937
6 TUBES, 1 BAND
BROWN BAKELITE $150
BLACK BAKELITE $175
IVORY PLASKON $275
RED PLASKON $750
GREEN PLASKON $750

LAFAYETTE E62 CA1940
CATALIN, 5 TUBES, 1 BAND
ONYX+ALABASTER $3000
ALABASTER $2000
ALABASTER+MAROON $2500
ALABASTER+TORTOISE $2800

LAFAYETTE S-107 CA1941
CATALIN, 5 TUBES, 1 BAND
YELLOW $750
BLACK+YELLOW $2500
MAROON+YELLOW $1800
YELLOW+MAROON $1500

LAFAYETTE E-74 CA1939
5 TUBES, 1 BAND
BROWN OR PAINTED BAKELITE $125
IVORY PLASKON $225

LAFAYETTE E-76 CA1939
6 TUBES, 1 BAND $75
BROWN OR PAINTED BAKELITE $40
IVORY PLASKON $75

LAFAYETTE FE-5 CA1940
BAKELITE, 6 TUBES, 1 BAND
BROWN OR PAINTED $125

LAFAYETTE FE1426 CA1942
BAKELITE, 5 TUBES, 1 BAND
BROWN OR PAINTED $150

LAFAYETTE Y-5 CA1948
5 TUBES, 1 BAND
BROWN OR PAINTED BAKELITE $75
IVORY PLASKON $135

LAFAYETTE J50M,Y CA1947
STYRENE, 5 TUBES, 1 BAND
MARBLED TAN $150
IVORY $75

LAFAYETTE JA-84 CA1940
6 TUBES, 2 BANDS
BROWN BAKELITE $40
IVORY PLASKON $75

LAFAYETTE JA-89 CA1940
BAKELITE, 5 TUBES, 1 BAND
BROWN OR PAINTED $75

LAFAYETTE JL-5 CA1948
BAKELITE, 5 TUBES, 1 BAND
BROWN OR PAINTED $20

LAFAYETTE LE-5 CA1953
BAKELITE, 4 TUBES, 1 BAND
BROWN OR PAINTED $40

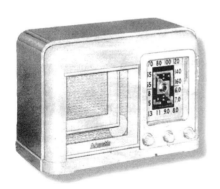

LAFAYETTE JS-187 CA1942
6 TUBES, 2 BANDS
BROWN OR PAINTED BAKELITE $75
IVORY PLASKON $135

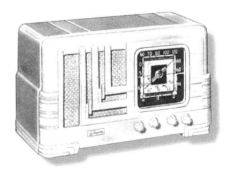

LAFAYETTE JS-189 CA1942
6 TUBES, 3 BANDS
BROWN OR PAINTED BAKELITE $110
IVORY PLASKON $175

LAFAYETTE MC-16 CA1948
4 TUBES, 1 BAND
BROWN OR PAINTED BAKELITE $75
IVORY PLASKON $135

LAFAYETTE T99 CA1940
4 TUBES, 1 BAND
BROWN OR PAINTED BAKELITE $60
IVORY PLASKON $110

LAFAYETTE MC10B,10Y CA1947
STYRENE, 5 TUBES, 1 BAND
BROWN OR PAINTED $40

LEAR 562 CA1947
BAKELITE, 5 TUBES, 1 BAND
BROWN OR PAINTED $30

MAGUIRE 561 CA1947
BAKELITE, 5 TUBES, 1 BAND
BROWN OR PAINTED $45

MAGUIRE 500D1 CA1948
BAKELITE, 5 TUBES, 1 BAND
BROWN OR PAINTED $25

MAJESTIC 250, 5LA5 CA1939
'ZEPHYR'
BAKELITE, 5 TUBES, 1 BAND
BROWN OR PAINTED $125
BLACK $150

MAJESTIC 1583W CA1950
'COIN-OP'
BAKELITE, 5 TUBES, 1 BAND
BROWN OR PAINTED $135

MAJESTIC 51 CA1947
5 TUBES, 1 BAND
BROWN OR PAINTED BAKELITE $100
IVORY PLASKON $150

MAJESTIC 5LA7 CA1947
BAKELITE, 6 TUBES, 1 BAND
BROWN OR PAINTED $115

MAJESTIC 7T11 CA1938
BAKELITE, 6 TUBES, 2 BANDS
BROWN OR PAINTED $125
BLACK $150

MAJESTIC 651 'TRIPLE FIN' CA1937
6 TUBES, 2 BANDS
BROWN BAKELITE $150, BLACK BAKELITE $200
IVORY PLASKON $325

MAJESTIC 5T CA1940
5 TUBES, 1 BAND, LIGHTED MIRROR DIAL
BAKELITE: BROWN $200, BLACK $250
PLASKON: IVORY $350, BEETLE $600

MAJESTIC 51 CA1937
5 TUBES, 1 BAND
BAKELITE: BROWN $150, BLACK $200
PLASKON: IVORY $275, BEETLE $400

MAJESTIC 511 CA1938
PLASKON+TENITE, 5 TUBES, 1 BAND
BEETLE $450
IVORY $375

MAJESTIC 5AK711 CA1947
PAINTED BAKELITE, 6 TUBES, 1 BAND
BLUE $135, RED $175, GREEN $150
GOLD $110, IVORY $100

MAJESTIC 9160 CA1955
BAKELITE, 5 TUBES, 1 BAND
BROWN OR PAINTED $40

MANTOLA 4775LQ CA1939
5 TUBES, 1 BAND
BAKELITE: BROWN $150, BLACK $175
IVORY PLASKON $275

MANTOLA 465-5LQ CA1939
5 TUBES, 1 BAND
BAKELITE: BROWN $175, BLACK $225
IVORY PLASKON $350

MARCONI 4T2 CA1959
STYRENE, 4 TUBES, 1 BAND
1388 $300

MANTOLA 339-6LQ CA1939
6 TUBES, 1 BAND
BLACK BAKELITE+CHROME $225
IVORY PLASKON+GOLD $300

MARCONI 153 CA1938
BAKELITE, 5 TUBES, 1 BAND
BROWN OR PAINTED $50

MARCONI 180,193 C.1940
BAKELITE, 5 TUBES, 1 BAND
BROWN OR PAINTED $100

MARCONI 230 CA1941
BAKELITE, 5 TUBES, 1 BAND
BROWN OR PAINTED $65

MARCONI 289 CA1950
BAKELITE, 5 TUBES, 1 BAND
BROWN OR PAINTED $75

MARCONI 218 CA1941
BAKELITE, 5 TUBES, 1 BAND
BROWN OR PAINTED $50

MARCONI 227 CA1941
BAKELITE, 5 TUBES, 1 BAND
BROWN OR PAINTED $50

MARCONI 258 CA1949
BAKELITE, 5 TUBES, 1 BAND
BROWN OR PAINTED $45

MARCONI 261 CA1948
BAKELITE+METAL, 5 TUBES, 1 BAND
BROWN OR PAINTED $40

MARCONI 216 CA1941
BAKELITE, 5 TUBES, 1 BAND
BROWN OR PAINTED $20

MARCONI 264 CA1948
BAKELITE, 5 TUBES, 1 BAND
BROWN+TAN $40

MARCONI 271 CA1949
BAKELITE, 5 TUBES, 1 BAND
BROWN OR PAINTED $30

MARCONI 275 CA1948
BAKELITE, 5 TUBES, 1 BAND
BROWN OR PAINTED $20

MARCONI 276 CA1958
BAKELITE, 9 TUBES, AM-FM
BROWN OR PAINTED $35

MARCONI 288 CA1948
5 TUBES, 1 BAND
BLACK BAKELITE+IVORY PLASKON $75

MARCONI 290 CA1950
BAKELITE, 4 TUBES, 1 BAND
$50

MARCONI 305 CA1950
BAKELITE, 5 TUBES, 1 BAND
BROWN OR PAINTED $30

MARCONI 317 CA1951
STYRENE, 4 TUBES, 1 BAND
BROWN $30, IVORY, BLACK $45
MAROON $50

MARCONI 359 CA1956
STYRENE, 5 TUBES, 1 BAND
$30

MARCONI 339 CA1952
BAKELITE, 5 TUBES, 1 BAND
$20

MARCONI 341 CA1955
BAKELITE, 6 TUBES, 1 BAND
$15

MARCONI 342 CA1954
STYRENE, 5 TUBES, 1 BAND
$25

MARCONI 349 CA1955
STYRENE, 5 TUBES, 1 BAND
$40

MARCONI 385 CA1955
STYRENE, 5 TUBES, 1 BAND
$30

MARCONI 417 CA1959
STYRENE, 5 TUBES, 1 BAND
$20

MARCONI 362 CA1953
STYRENE, 4 TUBES, 1 BAND
$45

MARCONI 425 CA1959
STYRENE, 5 TUBES, 1 BAND
$25

MARCONI 462 CA1959
STYRENE, 5 TUBES, 1 BAND
$30

MARCONI 472,482 C.1959
STYRENE, 5 TUBES, 1 BAND
$30

MECK 4C7, 237 CA1947
STYRENE, 4 TUBES, 1 BAND
BROWN OR PAINTED $50
BLACK $60

MECK 850 CA1947
4 TUBES, 1 BAND
BROWN BAKELITE $50
IVORY PLASKON $90

MECK CE500 CA1948
BAKELITE, 4 TUBES, 1 BAND
BROWN OR PAINTED $75

MECK CJ500 CA1948
BAKELITE, 5 TUBES, 1 BAND
BROWN OR PAINTED $20

MECK CP500 CA1948
'OLSON'
4 TUBES, 1 BAND
BROWN OR PAINTED BAKELITE $60
IVORY PLASKON $115

MECK CW500,DB602 CA1947
4 TUBES, 1 BAND
BROWN OR PAINTED BAKELITE $40
IVORY PLASKON $65

MEISSNER 6D CA1948
'BREWSTER'
BAKELITE, 5 TUBES, 1 BAND
BROWN OR PAINTED $50

MIDWEST JV-5 CA1950
STYRENE, 5 TUBES, 1 BAND, AC-DC
BROWN+TAN $75
SALMON+TAN $90

MIDWEST K-6 CA1940
6 TUBES, 2 BANDS
BROWN BAKELITE $175
IVORY PLASKON $325

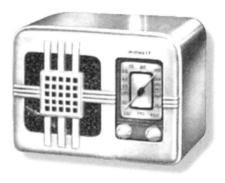

MIDWEST S-4, C.1940
BAKELITE, 4 TUBES, 1 BAND, DC
$30

MIRRORTONE 4B7 CA1947
4 TUBES, 1 BAND
BROWN OR PAINTED BAKELITE $60
IVORY PLASKON $115

MIRRORTONE 804 CA1948
4 TUBES, 1 BAND
BROWN BAKELITE $50
IVORY PLASKON $90

MISSION BELL CA1941
'TRU-DIAL'
BAKELITE, 5 TUBES, 1 BAND
BROWN OR PAINTED $125

MITCHELL 510 CA1951
STYRENE, 5 TUBES, 1 BAND
BROWN $25, IVORY $40

MOTOROLA 5C CA1951
'RADIO-LARM'
PAINTED BAKELITE
$50

MOTOROLA 5C13,5C22 CA1959
PLASKON, 5 TUBES, 1 BAND
BROWN $40, BLUE $115, PINK $115
TAN $90, YELLOW $150, LAVENDER $225

MOTOROLA 5C14,5C23 CA1959
STYRENE, 5 TUBES, 1 BAND
CORAL $60, GREEN $50
PINK $50, BROWN $35

MOTOROLA 5C21,56C5 CA1959
PLASKON, 5 TUBES, 1 BAND
BLUE $125, GREEN $135
PINK $125

MOTOROLA 5C24,25 C.1958
STYRENE, 5 TUBES, 1 BAND
BROWN $25, PINK $50

MOTOROLA 5C27 CA1958
PLASKON, 5 TUBES, 1 BAND
BROWN $50, IVORY $65, VIOLET $250
BLUE $145, AQUA $150

MOTOROLA 5H CA1951
BAKELITE
BROWN OR PAINTED IVORY $40
PAINTED GREEN OR MAROON $60

MOTOROLA 5L2U CA1950
STYRENE, 4 TUBES, 1 BAND
BROWN $40, IVORY $50, MAROON $75
ORANGE $125, RED $125, GREEN $75

MOTOROLA 5T12,A4G23 CA1958
STYRENE, 5 TUBES, 1 BAND
TAN $40, BLACK $50
GREEN $60, BROWN $30, RED $90

MOTOROLA 5J CA1951
'JEWEL BOX'
BROWN BAKELITE WITH
GREEN MARBLE TENITE GRILLE $125

MOTOROLA 5R CA1951
BAKELITE, 5 TUBES, 1 BAND
BROWN $30, GREEN $45, MAROON $50

MOTOROLA 52M CA1952
STYRENE, 4 TUBES, 1 BAND
BROWN $45, BLACK $60
GREEN $75, MAROON $75

MOTOROLA 5T11,5T23 CA1959
STYRENE 5 TUBES, 1 BAND
BROWN $30, IVORY $30
PINK $45, YELLOW $50

MOTOROLA 5T21,57A CA1957
STYRENE, 5 TUBES, 1 BAND
BROWN $25, BLACK $40
IVORY $40, RED $75

MOTOROLA 5T22M CA1958
'DRAGSTER'
STYRENE, 5 TUBES, 1 BAND
BROWN $80, BLACK $90, IVORY $90
YELLOW $150, ORANGE $160, RED $175

MOTOROLA 5X21 CA1953
BAKELITE+METAL, 5 TUBES, 1 BAND
BROWN OR PAINTED $110
BLACK $125

MOTOROLA 6X11 CA1950
BAKELITE, 6 TUBES, 1 BAND
BROWN OR PAINTED $60

MOTOROLA 5T27,57H CA1958
PLASKON, 5 TUBES, 1 BAND
BROWN $50, IVORY $75, BLACK $75
GREEN $150, VIOLET $250, LAVENDER $250

MOTOROLA 6C26,66C CA1958
PLASKON, 6 TUBES, 1 BAND
GREY $65
IVORY $60

MOTOROLA 6L1 CA1951
'TOWNE+COUNTRY'
STYRENE, 5 TUBES, 1 BAND
MAROON $75, GREEN $75

MOTOROLA 6T26,57H11 CA1958
PLASKON, 5-6 TUBES, 1 BAND
BROWN $40, IVORY $50, BLACK $60
GREEN $135, LAVENDER $225

MOTOROLA 7XM21 CA1950
PAINTED BAKELITE, 8 TUBES, AMFM
BROWN $50, IVORY $55
GREEN $75, MAROON $80

MOTOROLA 50X1,2 CA1941
BAKELITE, 5 TUBES, 1 BAND
BROWN $90
PAINTED IVORY $100

MOTOROLA 51A CA1939
BAKELITE, 5 TUBES, 1 BAND
BROWN $225
PAINTED IVORY $250

MOTOROLA 48L12,59L12 CA1948
STYRENE, 4 TUBES, 1 BAND, DC
MAROON $90, GREEN $90

MOTOROLA 50XC CA1940
'CIRCLE GRILLE'
CATALIN, 5 TUBES, 1 BAND
ALABASTER $5000
RED+ALABASTER $6000
GREEN+ALABASTER $7000
TURQUOISE+WHITE $7000

MOTOROLA 51X-15,16 CA1942
'S-GRILLE'
CATALIN, 5 TUBES, 1 BAND
BLACK+RED $6000
ALABASTER+GEEN $4500

MOTOROLA 52C CA1940
'VERTICAL GRILLE'
'FAN GRILLE'
CATALIN, 5 TUBES, 1 BAND
ALABASTER+TORTOISE $2700
GREEN+ALABASTER $3800
RED+ALABASTER $4000

MOTOROLA 51X11,58A11 CA1942
BAKELITE, 5 TUBES, 1 BAND
BROWN OR PAINTED IVORY $50

MOTOROLA 51X13,65X11 CA1942
BAKELITE, 5-6 TUBES, 1 BAND
BROWN OR PAINTED IVORY $40

MOTOROLA 52CW CA1952
PAINTED BAKELITE, 5 TUBES, 1 BAND
BROWN $30, IVORY $35, BLACK $35
MAROON $45, GREEN $45

MOTOROLA 52H CA1952
PAINTED BAKELITE, 5 TUBES, 1 BAND
BROWN $40, IVORY $50, BLACK $50
MAROON $60, GREEN $60

MOTOROLA 52R CA1952
PAINTED BAKELITE, 5 TUBES, 1 BAND
BROWN $60, IVORY $70, GREY $75
MAROON $90, GREEN $90, $YELLOW $125

MOTOROLA 52X13U CA1952
PAINTED BAKELITE, 5 TUBES, 1 BAND
BROWN $40, IVORY $50
MAROON $65

MOTOROLA 53C1 CA1953
PAINTED BAKELITE, 5 TUBES, 1 BAND
BROWN $30, TAN $35,
BLUE $60, GREEN $50

MOTOROLA 53C8 CA1953
STYRENE, 5 TUBES, 1 BAND
BROWN $20, IVORY $25
TAN $25, GREEN $40

MOTOROLA 53H 'JET' CA1954
PAINTED BAKELITE, 5 TUBES, 1 BAND
BLACK $150, GRAY $150,
GREEN $275, RED $225

MOTOROLA 53LC CA1955
STYRENE, 5 TUBES, 1 BAND
IVORY $125, BLACK $125
RED $175, GREEN $150

MOTOROLA 53R CA1953
PAINTED BAKELITE, 5 TUBES, 1 BAND
BROWN $35, IVORY $40, GREY $40
GREEN $65, YELLOW $100, RED $110

MOTOROLA 53X CA1953
PAINTED BAKELITE, 5 TUBES, 1 BAND
1549 BROWN $80,
TAN $90, GREEN $100,
ORANGE $125

MOTOROLA 54X CA1953
STYRENE, 5 TUBES, 1 BAND
BROWN $25, IVORY $30
GREEN $50

MOTOROLA 55A CA1955
STYRENE, 5 TUBES, 1 BAND
BROWN $25, BLACK $35
IVORY $35

MOTOROLA 55X11 CA1940
BAKELITE, 5 TUBES, 1 BAND
BROWN OR PAINTED IVORY $40

MOTOROLA 56CD CA1956
PLASKON, 5 TUBES, 1 BAND
BROWN $65, IVORY $100
AQUA $200, PINK $175

MOTOROLA 56CJ,62C CA1952
STYRENE, 5 TUBES, 1 BAND
BLACK $30, IVORY $30

MOTOROLA 56H CA1956
'TURBINE'
PLASKON, 5 TUBES, 1 BAND
BROWN $150, IVORY $200
AQUA $300, GREEN $300

MOTOROLA 56R CA1953
PLASKON, 5 TUBES, 1 BAND
BLACK $50, IVORY $60
GREEN $110, RED $125

MOTOROLA 52XAH1 CA1941
BAKELITE, 5 TUBES, 2 BANDS
BROWN+PAINTED IVORY $175

MOTOROLA 56X1 CA1941
BAKELITE, 5 TUBES, 1 BAND
BROWN OR PAINTED IVORY $110

MOTOROLA 56XA1 CA1941
BAKELITE, 5 TUBES, 1 BAND
BROWN OR PAINTED IVORY $35

MOTOROLA 57CS C1957
PLASKON, 5 TUBES, 1 BAND
BROWN $50 BLACK $60, IVORY $75
AQUA $150, GREEN $150, RED $175

MOTOROLA 57R CA1955
PLASKON, 5 TUBES, 1 BAND
BLACK $100, IVORY $125
AQUA $175, PURPLE $250

MOTOROLA 58R CA1949
PAINTED BAKELITE, 5 TUBES, 1 BAND
BROWN $50, IVORY $60, TAN $75
MAROON $80, GREEN $100, YELLOW $125

MOTOROLA 59H CA1950
BAKELITE, 5 TUBES, 1 BAND
BROWN OR PAINTED IVORY $50

MOTOROLA 57X CA1947
'PYRAMID'
BAKELITE, 5 TUBES, 1 BAND
BROWN OR PAINTED IVORY $75

MOTOROLA 58X CA1949
'PYRAMID'
BAKELITE, 5 TUBES, 1 BAND
BROWN OR PAINTED IVORY $75

MOTOROLA 59R CA1950
PAINTED BAKELITE, 5 TUBES, 1 BAND
BROWN $40, IVORY $45, TAN $50
GRAY $50, GREEN $75, RED $90

MOTOROLA 59X CA1950
BAKELITE, 5 TUBES, 1 BAND
BROWN OR PAINTED IVORY $50

MOTOROLA 61A CA1940
BAKELITE, 6 TUBES, 1 BAND
BROWN OR PAINTED IVORY $200

MOTOROLA 62L CA1952
STYRENE, 5 TUBES, 1 BAND
GREEN $50, MAROON $60
GREY $40

MOTOROLA 62X11(BROWN), 62X12(IVORY),
62X13(GREEN) CA1952
BAKELITE-PAINTED, 6 TUBES, 1 BAND
1569 BROWN $70,
IVORY $80, GREEN $110

**MOTOROLA 63C CA1954
'HELIPAD'**
PAINTED BAKELITE, 5 TUBES, 1 BAND,
BROWN $100, TAN $110, GREEN $150

MOTOROLA 63L CA1953
STYRENE, 5 TUBES, 1 BAND
GREEN $60, MAROON $65

MOTOROLA 63X CA1953
PAINTED BAKELITE, 6 TUBES, 1 BAND
BROWN $20, BLACK $25, IVORY $25, GREEN $40

MOTOROLA 67X CA1947
BAKELITE, 6 TUBES, 1 BAND
BROWN OR PAINTED IVORY $75

MOTOROLA 68T CA1949
BAKELITE, 6 TUBES, 1 BAND
BROWN OR PAINTED IVORY $35

MOTOROLA 68X CA1949
STYRENE, 6 TUBES, 1 BAND
BROWN+TAN $75
MAROON+TAN $125

MOTOROLA 69X CA1950
PAINTED BAKELITE, 6 TUBES, 1 BAND
BROWN $50, IVORY $60
GREEN $75

MOTOROLA 79XM CA1949
BAKELITE, 7 TUBES, AM-FM
BROWN OR PAINTED IVORY $175

MOTOROLA AR1 CA1959
STYRENE, 5 TUBES, 1 BAND
TAN $35, WHITE $30

MOTOROLA A9 CA1960
STYRENE, 5 TUBES, 1 BAND
TAN $30, IVORY $25

MOTOROLA A12 CA1960
STYRENE, 6 TUBES, 1 BAND
TAN $40, BLACK $50
BLUE $75, RED $100

MOTOROLA A23 CA1960
STYRENE, 5 TUBES, 1 BAND
BROWN $25, IVORY $30

MOTOROLA AX5 CA1961
STYRENE, TRANSISTORS
TAN $20, PINK $40

MOTOROLA B1,B2 CA1960
STYRENE, 8 TUBES, AMFM
TAN $30, GRAY $30
BLUE $45

MOTOROLA B3 CA1960
STYRENE, 8 TUBES, AMFM
IVORY $30, TAN $30
BLUE $45, PINK $45

MOTOROLA C11 CA1960
STYRENE, 5 TUBES, 1 BAND
IVORY $20, GRAY $25
TAN $25

MOTOROLA C15 CA1960
STYRENE, 5 TUBES, 1 BAND
IVORY $25, TAN $25
RED $75

MUSICAIRE CA1955
STYRENE, 5 TUBES, 1 BAND
IVORY $20, BLACK $25
YELLOW $60

NAMCO 601 CA1946
CATALIN, 5 TUBES, 1 BAND
GREEN $300
BLUE $4000

NORTHERN ELECTRIC 518 CA1957
STYRENE, 5 TUBES, 1 BAND
$45

NORTHERN ELECTRIC 548 CA1957
STYRENE, 5 TUBES, 1 BAND
$20

NORTHERN ELECTRIC 598 CA1957
STYRENE, 5 TUBES, 1 BAND
$25

NORTHERN ELECTRIC 607 CA1957
STYRENE, 5 TUBES, 1 BAND
$75

NORTHERN ELECTRIC 1101 CA1957
STYRENE, 5 TUBES, 1 BAND
$25

NORTHERN ELECTRIC 1201 CA1957
STYRENE, 5 TUBES, 1 BAND
$30

NORTHERN ELECTRIC 1102 CA1957
STYRENE, 5 TUBES, 1 BAND
$30

NORTHERN ELECTRIC 1102 CA1957
'EXTENSION SPEAKER'
$30

NORTHERN ELECTRIC 5410 CA1958
STYRENE, 4 TUBES, 1 BAND
$60

NORTHERN ELECTRIC 5400 CA1948
'BABY CHAMP'
5 TUBES, 1 BAND
PAINTED BAKELITE+IVORY TENITE

NORTHERN ELECTRIC 5500 CA1958
'SKY CHAMP'
STYRENE, 5 TUBES, 1 BAND
$50

NORTHERN ELECTRIC 5700 CA1953
STYRENE, 5 TUBES, 1 BAND
$45

NORTHERN ELECTRIC 5508 CA1958
'BULLET'
PAINTED BAKELITE, 5 TUBES, 1 BAND
$125

NORTHERN ELECTRIC 5708 CA1954
PAINTED BAKELITE, 5 TUBES, 1 BAND
$75

NORTHERN ELECTRIC B4000 CA1947
'RAINBOW GRILLE'
PAINTED BAKELITE, 5 TUBES, 1 BAND
BROWN $125, IVORY FINISH $75
METALLIC BLUE $100, METALLIC GREEN $100

OLYMPIC 6-501,7-421 CA1946
BAKELITE, 5 TUBES, 1 BAND
BROWN OR PAINTED IVORY $90
BLACK $110

OLYMPIC 6-505 CA1946
BAKELITE, 5 TUBES, 1 BAND
BLACK $75, PAINTED IVORY $60

OLYMPIC 6-601 CA1946
BAKELITE, 5 TUBES, 1 BAND
BLACK $40, PAINTED IVORY $25

OLYMPIC 557 CA1958
STYRENE, 5 TUBES, 1 BAND
TAN $50, AQUA $75
CORAL $90

OLYMPIC CA1958
STYRENE, 5 TUBES, 1 BAND
BLACK $35, IVORY $30
RED $60

ORIOLE 3-A2 CA1938
6 TUBES+MAGIC EYE, 3 BANDS
BLACK BAKELITE $175
IVORY PLASKON $250

ORIOLE PC1365 CA1937
6 TUBES, 2 BANDS
BAKELITE: BROWN $100, BLACK $125
PLASKON: IVORY $175, RED $650
BEETLE $350

ORIOLE 30C-66 CA1953
BAKELITE, 5 TUBES, 1 BAND
$25

ORIOLE 36B-17 CA1956
BAKELITE, 5 TUBES, 1 BAND
1646 $40

ORIOLE 36B-18 CA1956
STYRENE, 6 TUBES, 1 BAND
MARBELED TAN $75

ORIOLE 36B-19 CA1956
STYRENE, 6 TUBES, 1 BAND
$50

ORIOLE 513-5A CA1938
BAKELITE, 5 TUBES, 1 BAND
BROWN OR PAINTED $200

ORIOLE 516-5C CA1938
BAKELITE, 5 TUBES, 1 BAND
BROWN OR PAINTED $60

ORIOLE C3-101 CA1940
BAKELITE, 5 TUBES, 1 BAND
BROWN OR PAINTED $135

ORIOLE C3-137 CA1940
BAKELITE, 5 TUBES, 2 BANDS
BROWN OR PAINTED $70

ORIOLE C3-151 CA1941
4 TUBES, 1 BAND
BROWN BAKELITE $80
IVORY PLASKON $140

ORIOLE R-3126 CA1941
BAKELITE, 6 TUBES, 2 BANDS
BROWN OR PAINTED $60

ORIOLE R2825 CA1942
BAKELITE, 5 TUBES, 1 BAND, AC-DC
BROWN OR PAINTED $40

ORIOLE R2828 CA1942
5 TUBES, 1 BAND, AC-DC
BROWN OR PAINTED $50

ORIOLE R4102 CA1940
BAKELITE-PLASKON, 6 TUBES, 2 BANDS
1686 BROWN $150,
IVORY $225

ORIOLE R3111 CA1940
5 TUBES, 1 BAND
BROWN OR PAINTED $150

PACIFIC 1A1,15A1 CA1937
5 TUBES, 2 BANDS
BAKELITE: BROWN $60, BLACK $75
PLASKON: IVORY $125, RED $600

PACIFIC 3A2,20A2 CA1937
5 TUBES, 2 BANDS
BAKELITE: BROWN $100, BLACK $125
PLASKON: IVORY $175, RED $650

PACKARD-BELL 550 CA1948
BAKELITE, 5 TUBES, 1 BAND
BROWN OR PAINTED $75

PACKARD-BELL 5D,5FP CA1946
5 TUBES, 2 BANDS
BAKELITE: BROWN $75
PLASKON: IVORY $125,
LT BLUE $500, LT GREEN $600

PACKARD-BELL 5R1 CA1956
STYRENE, 5 TUBES, 1 BAND
IVORY $25, BLACK $30
GREEN $40

PACKARD-BELL 501 CA1938
5 TUBES, 1 BAND
BAKELITE: BROWN $65, MAROON $100
IVORY PLASKON $125

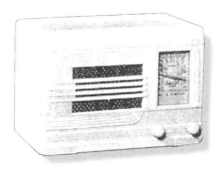

PACKARD-BELL "KOMPAK" CA1938
5 TUBES, 1 BAND
BROWN BAKELITE $125
PLASKON: IVORY $200, RED $650,
BLUE $700

PHILCO 40-90,PT-30 CA1941
BAKELITE, 5 TUBES, 1 BAND
BROWN OR PAINTED $60

PHILCO 46-131,49-100 CA1949
BAKELITE, 5 TUBES, 1 BAND
BROWN OR PAINTED $40

PHILCO 49-500,PT-91 CA1949
BAKELITE, 5 TUBES, 1 BAND
BROWN OR PAINTED $30

PHILCO 46-250,49-500,PT-2 CA1946
BAKLELITE, 5 TUBES, 1 BAND
BROWN OR PAINTED $30

PHILCO 48-420,49-900 CA1948
'HIPPO'
BAKELITE, 5 TUBES, 1 BAND
BROWN OR PAINTED $150
BLACK $175

PHILCO 47-902 CA1947
BAKELITE, 5 TUBES, 1 BAND
BROWN+TAN $75
MAROON+TAN $125

PHILCO 49-501 CA1949
'BOOMERANG'
BAKELITE, 5 TUBES, 1 BAND
BROWN OR PAINTED $375

PHILCO 49-503 CA1949
'FLYING WEDGE'
STYRENE, 5 TUBES, 1 BAND
BLACK $200, BROWN $150
MAROON $225, TEAL $300

PHILCO 49-505 CA1949A
BAKELITE, 5 TUBES, 1 BAND
BROWN OR PAINTED $75

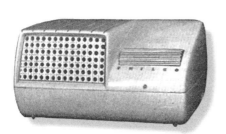

PHILCO 49-901 CA1949
'SECRETARY'
UNIQUE SINGLE CONTROL OPERATION VIA FOOT ROLLER
BAKELITE, 5 TUBES, 1 BAND
BROWN OR PAINTED $125, BLACK $150

PHILCO 904 CA1949
STYRENE, 6 TUBES, 2 BANDS
BROWN $35, BLACK $40
MAROON $60

PHILCO 49-905, 50-925
905 CA1949
BAKELITE, 6 TUBES, AM-FM
BROWN OR PAINTED $30

PHILCO 906 CA1949
BAKELITE, 8 TUBES, AM-FM
BROWN OR PAINTED $40

PHILCO 50-520,PT-540 CA1952
BAKELITE, 5 TUBES, 1 BAND
BROWN OR PAINTED $20

PHILCO 50-522 CA1952
BAKELITE, 5 TUBES, 1 BAND
BROWN OR PAINTED $25

PHILCO 50-526,PT-542 CA1950
BAKELITE, 5 TUBES, 1 BAND
BLACK $75, BROWN OR PAINTED IVORY $50
PAINTED MAROON $100

PHILCO 50-527,51-538,PT-544 CA1951
BAKELITE, 5 TUBES, 1 BAND
BROWN OR PAINTED $75

PHILCO 50-921,52-941 CA1952
BAKELITE, 6 TUBES, 1 BAND
BROWN OR PAINTED $65
BLACK $75

PHILCO 605 CA1949
BAKELITE, 6 TUBES, 1 BAND
$50

PHILCO 640 CA1952
STYRENE, 5 TUBES, 1 BAND
RED $50

PHILCO 641 CA1952
STYRENE, 6 TUBES, 1 BAND
GREEN $65, BLUE $75
RED $75, TAN $55

PHILCO 52-643,53-656 CA1952
STYRENE, 6 TUBES, 1 BAND
TAN $30

PHILCO 52-940 CA1952
BAKELITE, 5 TUBES, 1 BAND
BROWN OR PAINTED IVORY $100
BLACK $125

PHILCO 944 CA1952
BAKELITE, 7 TUBES, AM-FM
BROWN OR PAINTED $20

PHILCO 547 CA1953
BAKELITE, 5 TUBES, 1 BAND
BROWN OR PAINTED $25

PHILCO 550 CA1953
BAKELITE, 5 TUBES, 1 BAND
BROWN OR PAINTED $20

PHILCO 561 CA1953
STYRENE, 5 TUBES, 1 BAND
BROWN $50, TAN $60
WHEAT $75, OLIVE $75

PHILCO 562 CA1953
STYRENE, 5 TUBES, 1 BAND
$20

PHILCO 564 CA1953
STYRENE, 5 TUBES, 1 BAND
$30

PHILCO 53-563 CA1953
'SPLIT LEVEL'
BAKELITE, 5 TUBES, 1 BAND
BLACK $150, BROWN $110
PAINTED: RED $140, IVORY $120, MAROON $130

PHILCO 53-566,PT-548 CA1952
BAKELITE, 5 TUBES, 1 BAND
BLACK $150, BROWN $135
PAINTED IVORY $140

PHILCO 53-700 CA1953
BAKELITE, 5 TUBES, 1 BAND
BROWN OR PAINTED $20

PHILCO 53-702,54-714 CA1953
BAKELITE, 5 TUBES, 1 BAND
BROWN OR PAINTED $25

PHILCO 53-956 CA1953
BAKELITE, 7 TUBES, AM-FM
BROWN OR PAINTED $20

PHILCO 55-590,56-814 CA1956
STYRENE, 5 TUBES, 1 BAND
BROWN $20, IVORY $25, GREY $40
GREEN $50, RED $75

PHILCO 717 CA1955
STYRENE, 4 TUBES, ONE BAND
BROWN $20, IVORY $25

PHILCO 56-740 CA1956
STYRENE, 5 TUBES, 1 BAND
IVORY $20, PINK $40

PHILCO 56-808 CA1956
BAKELITE, 5 TUBES, 1 BAND
BROWN OR PAINTED $15

PHILCO 56-812 CA1956
STYRENE, 5 TUBES, 1 BAND
BROWN $20, PINK $40
YELLOW $75, ORANGE $75

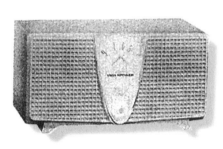

PHILCO 56-816 CA1956
STYRENE, 5 TUBES, 1 BAND
BROWN $40, IVORY $50
TAN $60
'

PHILCO 57-809 CA1957
STYRENE, 5 TUBES, 1 BAND
BROWN $15, IVORY $30,

PHILCO 58-681 CA1958
STYRENE, 5 TUBES, 1 BAND
IVORY $20, TAN $20
PINK $40, AQUA $45

PHILCO 58-750 CA1958
STYRENE, 5 TUBES, 1 BAND
IVORY, TAN $25
PINK $40

PHILCO 58-754 CA1958
STYRENE, 5 TUBES, 1 BAND
IVORY $75, GREY $90

PHILCO 58-758 CA1958
STYRENE, 5 TUBES, 1 BAND
TAN $70, PINK $100

PHILCO 58-974 CA1958
STYRENE, 7 TUBES, AM-FM
$30

PHILCO 59-749 CA1959
STYRENE, 5 TUBES, 1 BAND
BROWN $40, IVORY $50
PINK $75

PHILCO 59-751 CA1959
STYRENE, 5 TUBES, 1 BAND
IVORY $60,
PINK $75, BLUE $85

PHILCO 59-824,60-834 CA1959
STYRENE, 5 TUBES, 1 BAND
IVORY $30, PINK $50
AQUA $75

PHILCO 59-753,60-763 CA1959
STYRENE, 5 TUBES, 1 BAND
IVORY, BLACK $20,
PINK $45, GREEN $60, BLUE $60

PHILCO 59-755,60-764 CA1959
STYRENE, 5 TUBES, 1 BAND
IVORY $20,
BLUE $70, PINK $65

PHILCO 59-820 CA1959
STYRENE, 5 TUBES, 1 BAND
IVORY $30,
YELLOW $75

PHILCO 59-826,60-835 CA1959
STYRENE, 5 TUBES, 1 BAND
IVORY $25, ORANGE $90, BLUE $75
BROWN $15, GREY $25

PHILCO 59-828 CA1959
STYRENE, 5 TUBES, 1 BAND
IVORY $20, BROWN $15

PHILCO 59-963 CA1959
STYRENE, 6 TUBES, 1 BAND
IVORY $25, BROWN $20

PHILCO 59-995 CA1959
STYRENE, 7 TUBES, AM-FM
TAN $20, GRAY $25
PINK $40, AQUA $45

PHILCO 60-772 CA1960
STYRENE, 5 TUBES, 1 BAND
TAN $20, PINK $40
BLUE $45

PHILCO 61-783 CA1961
STYRENE, 5 TUBES, 1 BAND
TAN $20, PINK $40

PHILCO 61-852 CA1961
STYRENE, 5 TUBES, 1 BAND
BROWN $20, PINK $45
IVORY $25, BLACK $25

PHILCO 61-847,62-860 CA1961
STYRENE, 5 TUBES, 1 BAND
BLACK $20, TAN $20,
BROWN $15

PHILCO 62-777 CA1961
STYRENE, 5 TUBES, 1 BAND
IVORY $25

**PHILCO 61-785, 62-797 CA1961
'DOUBLE PREDICTA'**
STYRENE, 5 TUBES, 1 BAND
BLACK $200, IVORY $175

**PHILCO 60-765,J775-124 CA1960
'PREDICTA'**
5 TUBES, 1 BAND
BLACK $250
IVORY $225

PHILCO 64-709 CA1964
STYRENE, 5 TUBES, 1 BAND,
BLACK $20, WHITE $20

**PHILCO T1000-124 CA1959
'TRIPLE PREDICTA'**
STYRENE, 6 TRANSISTORS, DC
BLACK $250, IVORY $225

PHILCO 64-714 CA1964
5 TUBES, 1 BAND,
TAN $20, PINK $45
AQUA $50

PHILCO T-600 CA1959
STYRENE, TRANSISTORIZED, 1 BAND
$75

PHILCO B649 CA1953
STYRENE, 4 TUBES, 1 BAND, DC
MAROON $50, GREEN $50
TAN $40

PHILCO PT-87 CA1941
5 TUBES, 1 BAND
MARBLED TAN TENITE $125

PHILCO PT-25 CA1942
BAKELITE, 5 TUBES, 1 BAND
BROWN OR PAINTED IVORY $60

PHILCO PT-27,TH-16 CA1939
BAKELITE, 5 TUBES, 1 BAND
BROWN OR PAINTED IVORY $60

PHILCO PT-46 CA1938
5 TUBES, 1 BAND
BROWN OR PAINTED BAKELITE $125
IVORY PLASKON $200

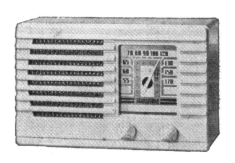

PHILCO TP-4 CA1939
BAKELITE, 5 TUBES, 1 BAND
BROWN OR PAINTED IVORY $60

PHILCO TH-7 CA1939
BAKELITE, 5 TUBES, 1 BAND
BROWN OR PAINTED IVORY $65

PHILCO TP-7,TP-10 CA1939
'COLLEGE'
BAKELITE, 5 TUBES, 1 BAND
PAINTED BAKELITE+IVORY TENITE $350
BAKELITE+MARBLED TAN TENITE $400
NOTE: MARKETED TO COLLEGE STUDENTS AND OFFERED PAINTED
IN A WIDE VARIETY OF COLLEGE COLORS

PHILCO TP-11,PT67 CA1939
BAKELITE+TENITE GRILLE
5 TUBES, 1 BAND
$500

PHILCO TP-20 CA1939
5 TUBES, 1 BAND
BLACK BAKELITE+IVORY PLASKON $5,000
BLACK BAKELITE+LT BLUE PLASKON $7,500

PHILCO CANADA 182 C.1955
BAKELITE, 5 TUBES, 1 BAND
$60

PHILHARMONIC CA1951
STYRENE, 5 TUBES, 1 BAND
IVORY $40, BLACK $50
PINK $100, YELLOW $125

PHILIPS 905 CA1949
BAKELITE, 5 TUBES, 1 BAND
BROWN OR PAINTED $50

PHILIPS B2-C10U CA1958
STYRENE, 5 TUBES, 1 BAND
TAN $100, ORANGE $145
AQUA $125, CORAL $135

PHILIPS CM23L CA1952
BAKELITE, 5 TUBES, 1 BAND
BROWN OR PAINTED $30

PHILIPS B1C12U CA1958
STYRENE, 5 TUBES, 1 BAND
AQUA $115, CORAL $115
TAN $90, YELLOW $125

PHILIPS B1C13U CA1959
STYRENE, 5 TUBES, 1 BAND
AQUA $125, CORAL $125
TAN $100, YELLOW $140

PILOT B1 CA1941
5 TUBES, 1 BAND
BROWN BAKELITE $75
IVORY PLASKON $125

PILOT BG562 CA1938
7 TUBES, 2 BANDS
BROWN BAKELITE $1000
BLACK BAKELITE $1200
IVORY PLASKON $1500

PILOT 'JUNIOR' CA1941
6 TUBES, 2 BANDS
IVORY PLASKON+BLACK BAKELITE $400
ALL IVORY $250

PILOT X203A CA1936
7 TUBES, 2 BANDS
BROWN BAKELITE $1000
BLACK BAKELITE $1200
IVORY PLASKON $1500

PILOT 'MAJOR MAESTRO CA1939
5 TUBES, 1 BAND
BROWN BAKELITE $90
IVORY PLASKON $135

RAULAND 546T 'LYRIC' CA1947
BAKELITE, 5 TUBES, 1 BAND
BROWN OR PAINTED $40

RADOLEK B1765 CA1940
5 TUBES, 1 BAND
BROWN OR PAINTED $350

RADOLEK B17660 CA1939
BAKELITE, 5 TUBES, 1 BAND
BAKELITE: BROWN $175, BLACK $200
IVORY PLASKON $275

RADOLEK B17678 CA1939
BAKELITE, 5 TUBES, 1 BAND
BROWN OR PAINTED $175
BLACK $200

RADOLEK B17676 CA1939
BAKELITE, 6 TUBES, 1 BAND
BROWN OR PAINTED $200
BLACK $225

RADOLEK C17520 CA1940
5 TUBES, 1 BAND
BROWN OR PAINTED $100
BLACK $125

RADOLEK C17573 CA1940
6 TUBES, 1 BAND
BROWN OR PAINTED $125

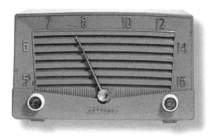

RAYTHEON 5R-12R CA1957
STYRENE, TRANSISTOR, 1 BAND
$50

RCA 1AX,46X21 CA1940
BAKELITE, 5 TUBES, 1BAND
1981 BROWN $45
IVORY $50

RCA 1R81,3RF91 CA1952
'WOODARD'
BAKELITE, 5 TUBES, 1 BAND
$25

RCA 1X51 CA1953
'BLAINE'
STYRENE, 5 TUBES, 1 BAND
TAN $30, RED $50

RCA 1X591 CA1953
'GLADWIN'
BAKELITE, 5 TUBES, 1 BAND
$50

RCA 4C531 CA1952
'REVEILLE'
BAKELITE, 5 TUBES, 1 BAND
$20

RCA 2C511,2G511 CA1953
STYRENE, 5 TUBES, 1 BAND
BLACK $40, IVORY $35, RED $70
TAN $30, GRAY $30

RCA 2R51 CA1953
HENRY DREYFUSS DESIGN
STYRENE, 5 TUBES, 1 BAND
BLACK+TAN $125
TAN+IVORY $110

RCA 2X621 CA1952
BAKELITE, 5 TUBES, 1 BAND
$25

RCA 2XF91 CA1953
STYRENE, 5 TUBES, 1 BAND
MAROON $50, IVORY $35, GREEN $50
RED $90, TAN $40

RCA 3X521 CA1954
STYRENE, 5 TUBES, 1 BAND
$15

**RCA 4C671,4C531 CA1952
'PROMPTER'**
STYRENE, 5 TUBES, 1 BAND
$30

**RCA 4V541 CA1952
'SLUMBERETTE'**
BAKELITE, 5 TUBES, 1 BAND
$25

**RCA 4X551 CA1955
'CREIGHTON'**
STYRENE, 5 TUBES, 1 BAND
BLACK $100, BROWN $75
IVORY $100, RED $125

**RCA 4X641 CA1954
'DRISCOLL'**
STYRENE, 5 TUBES, 1 BAND
$15

**RCA 5C581 CA1954
'DEBONAIRE'**
STYRENE
BLACK $60

RCA 5Q5,5Q55,6Q1 CA1939
BAKELITE, 5 TUBES, 3 BANDS
BROWN OR PAINTED $75

RCA 9SX CA1939
'NIPPER'
NORMAN BEL GEDDES DESIGN
5 TUBES, 1 BAND
BROWN BAKELITE $300
BEETLE PLASKON $500
BLUE+BEETLE $1200
GREEN+BEETLE $1500
RED+BEETLE $1500

RCA 9TX4 CA1939
'LITTLE NIPPER'
NORMAN BEL GEDDES DESIGN
CATALIN, 5 TUBES, 1 BAND
YELLOW+RED $1500
GREEN+IVORY $2000

RCA 9X11 CA1938
'W GRILLE'
CATALIN, 4 TUBES, 1 BAND
GREEN $2200
BLACK $1500
IVORY $1200
BROWN $1000

RCA 5X5,9TX21,40X30,45X1 CA1939
5 TUBES, 1 BAND
BROWN OR PAINTED BAKELITE $75
IVORY PLASKON $150

**RCA Z5-X-560 CA1954
'GREENWICH'**
STYRENE, 5 TUBES, 1 BAND
BLACK $40, RED $70

RCA 8X541 CA1949
BAKELITE, 5 TUBES, 1 BAND
$40

RCA 8X54 CA1948
BAKELITE, 5 TUBES, 1 BAND
BROWN OR PAINTED $60

RCA 8R72 CA1947
BAKELITE, 7 TUBES, AM-FM
$20

RCA 8X71,X711 CA1947
BAKELITE, 7 TUBES, AM-FM
$25

RCA 6XF9 CA1955
'LINDSAY'
STYRENE, 8 TUBES, AM-FM
BLACK $20

RCA 8X681 CA1948
HENRY DREYFUSS DESIGN
BAKELITE, 6 TUBES, 2 BANDS
$225

RCA 9BX5 CA1949
BAKELITE, 5 TUBES, 1 BAND, AC-DC
$45

RCA 9BX56 CA1949
STYRENE, 5 TUBES, 1 BAND
$60

RCA 9X641,9X651 CA1949
BAKELITE, 6 TUBES, 1 BAND
BROWN OR PAINTED $30

RCA 9XL1F CA1951
STYRENE, 5 TUBES, 1 BAND
CIGARETTE LIGHTER ON TOP
IVORY $60, PINK $75

RCA 9X561 CA1949
BAKELITE, 5 TUBES, 1 BAND
$50

RCA 9-X-571 CA1950
'BULLHORN'
BAKELITE, 5 TUBES, 1 BAND
$75

RCA 10X,26X,Q10 CA1940
BAKELITE, 5 TUBES, 1 BAND
5 TUBES, 1 BAND
BROWN OR PAINTED $20

RCA 56X CA1942
BAKELITE, 6 TUBES, 1 BAND
BROWN OR PAINTED $20

RCA 66X2,Q103 CA1942
BAKELITE, 5 TUBES, 3 BANDS
BROWN OR PAINTED $30

RCA Q32 CA1942
BAKELITE, 6 TUBES, 5 BANDS
$35

RCA 61-8,65X-8,9,64F,65X CA1946
BAKELITE, 5 TUBES, 1 BAND
$20

RCA 66X11 CA1948
BAKELITE, 5 TUBES, 1 BAND
$25

RCA 68R1 CA1948
BAKELITE, 8 TUBES, AM-FM
$20

RCA 75X1 CA1948
BAKELITE WITH GOLD FACE
$40

RCA B411 CA1950
STYRENE, 4 TUBES, 1 BAND, DC
MARBELED BROWN $75

RCA BX55 CA1950
4 TUBES, 1 BAND, AC-DC
$30

RCA 9TX1,2 CA1939
'LITTLE NIPPER'
NORMAN BEL GEDDES DESIGN
5 TUBES, 1 BAND
BROWN BAKELITE $150
IVORY PLASKON $275

RCA 66X8 CA1947
CATALIN, 5 TUBES, 1 BAND
MARBELED RED $1000
SOLID BLACK $750

RCA 96X14 CA1939
'VASSOS'
JOHN VASSOS DESIGN
6 TUBES, 1 BAND
BROWN BAKELITE $350
IVORY PLASKON $500
BROWN BAKELITE+TAN PLASKON $600

**RCA PX600 CA1952
'GLOBETROTTER'**
BAKELITE, 5 TUBES, 1 BAND
$30

RCA Q2 CA1939
BAKELITE, 6 TUBES, 2 BANDS
$30

RCA Q121 CA1942
BAKELITE, 6 TUBES, 5 BANDS
$20

RCA X551 CA1950
BAKELITE, 5 TUBES, 1 BAND
BROWN OR PAINTED $50

RCA CANADA 523 CA1953
BAKELITE, 5 TUBES, 1 BAND
$50

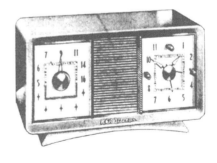

RCA CANADA C528 CA1957
STYRENE, 5 TUBES, 1 BAND
$25

**RCA CANADA CA1951
'CHANTICLEER'**
STYRENE, 5 TUBES, 1 BAND
2176 $30

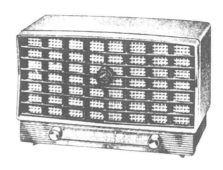

RCA CANADA X110 CA1957
STYRENE, 5 TUBES, 1 BAND
$20

RCA CANADA X310 CA1958
STYRENE, 5 TUBES, 1 BAND
$75

**RCA CANADA CA1948
'BABY NIPPER'**
NORMAN BEL GEDDES DESIGN
BAKELITE, 5 TUBES, 1 BAND
BROWN OR PAINTED $125

**RCA CANADA CA1952
'NIPPER II'**
STYRENE, 5 TUBES, 1 BAND
BROWN $45, IVORY $60

**RCA CANADA CA1956
'NIPPER IV,V'**
STYRENE, 5 TUBES, 1 BAND
$40

REGAL 271 CA1954
STYRENE, 5 TUBES, 1 BAND
$25

REGAL 471 CA1954
STYRENE, 5 TUBES, 1 BAND
$20

REGAL 575 CA1954
STYRENE, 4 TUBES, 1 BAND
$45

REGAL 702 CA1954
STYRENE, 5 TUBES, 1 BAND
IVORY $50, BLACK $60
MAROON $75

REGAL 472 CA1954
STYRENE, 4 TUBES, 1 BAND
IVORY $75, BLACK $75
MAROON $90

REGAL C473 CA1954
STYRENE, 4 TUBES, 1 BAND
IVORY $90, BLACK $90
MAROON $125

REGAL 707 CA1954
BAKELITE, 5 TUBES, 1 BAND
BROWN OR PAINTED $20

REGAL 718 CA1954
BAKELITE, 6 TUBES, 2 BANDS
BROWN OR PAINTED $30

REGAL 801 CA1947
BAKELITE, 6 TUBES, 1 BAND, AC-DC
BROWN OR PAINTED $20

REGAL 1877 CA1954
STYRENE, 4 TUBES, 1 BAND
$40

REGAL C527 CA1954
STYRENE, 5 TUBES, 1 BAND
IVORY $50, BLACK $60
MAROON $80

REMLER 5 'SCOTTY' CA1941
BAKELITE, 5 TUBES, 1 BAND
$225

REMLER 'SCOTTY' 26 CA1934
5 TUBES, 1 BAND
BLACK BAKELITE+IVORY PLASKON $800
IVORY PLASKON+BLACK BAKELITE $1000

REMLER 'SCOTTIE' 40 CA1936
BLACK BAKELITE+IVORY PLASKON $650
IVORY PLASKON+BLACK BAKELITE $800

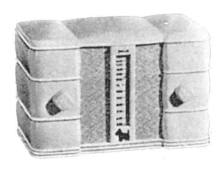

REMLER 'SCOTTIE' 46 CA1937
5 TUBES, 2 BANDS
IVORY PLASKON $600
BLACK BAKELITE+IVORY PLASKON $800

REMLER 'SCOTTY' CA1947
BAKELITE, 5 TUBES, 1 BAND
BROWN OR PAINTED BAKELITE $200
BLACK BAKELITE $250
IVORY PLASKON $375

REMLER 51 'SKIPPER' CA1936
5 TUBES, 1 BAND
BAKELITE: BROWN $150, BLACK $175
PLASKON: IVORY $250, BEETLE $400

REMLER 54 CA1938
5 TUBES, 1 BAND
BAKELITE: BROWN $125, BLACK $150
IVORY PLASKON $225

RETS MIDGET KIT CA1948
5 TUBES, 1 BAND
BROWN OR PAINTED BAKELITE $50
IVORY PLASKON $90

ROGERS R201U CA1955
STYRENE, 5 TUBES, 1 BAND
IVORY $40, BLACK $45
GREEN $60, YELLOW $100

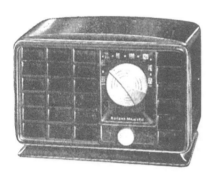

ROGERS 120 CA1949
BAKELITE, 5 TUBES, 1 BAND
BROWN OR PAINTED $30

ROGERS R151 CA1950
BAKELITE, 5 TUBES, 1 BAND
BROWN OR PAINTED $50

ROGERS R202U CA1959
STYRENE, 5 TUBES, 1 BAND
BROWN $45, IVORY $60, BLACK $60
ORANGE $125, YELLOW $110, AQUA $120

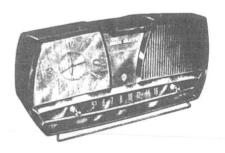

ROGERS R203U CA1959
STYRENE, 5 TUBES, 1 BAND
BROWN $45, IVORY $60, BLACK $60
ORANGE $125, YELLOW $110, AQUA $120

SENTINAL 124 CA1939
BAKELITE, 5 TUBES, 1 BAND
BROWN OR PAINTED $110
BLACK $125

SENTINAL 212 CA1941
5 TUBES, 1 BAND
BAKELITE: BROWN $60, BLACK $75
PLASKON: IVORY $125, BEETLE $250

SENTINAL 137 CA1939
4 TUBES, 1 BAND, DC
BAKELITE: BROWN $50, BLACK $70,
MAROON $125
IVORY PLASKON $100

SENTINAL 194,226,309 CA1940
BAKELITE, 5 TUBES, 1 BAND
BROWNOR PAINTED $60

SENTINAL 195 CA1940
5 TUBES, 1 BAND
BAKELITE BROWN $110, BLACK $125
PLASKON: IVORY $175, BEETLE $350

SENTINAL 218 CA1941
5 TUBES, 1 BAND
BAKELITE BROWN $60, BLACK $75
PLASKON: IVORY $125, BEETLE $300

SENTINAL 216 CA1939
5 TUBES, 1 BAND
BAKELITE: BROWN $50, MAROON $75
IVORY PLASKON $75

SENTINAL 298,314 CA1947
BAKELITE, 5 TUBES, 1 BAND
BROWN OR PAINTED $35

SENTINAL 302 CA1948
BAKELITE, 8 TUBES, AM+FM
BROWN OR PAINTED $70

SENTINAL 313 CA1948
BAKELITE, 5 TUBES, 1 BAND
BROWN OR PAINTED $20

SENTINAL 316P CA1948
STYRENE, 4 TUBES, 1 BAND
BLACK $30, IVORY $30
GREEN $45, MAROON $45

SENTINAL 331W CA1949
BAKELITE, 5 TUBES, 1 BAND
BROWN OR PAINTED $30

SENTINAL 177U CA1940
CATALIN, 5 TUBES, 1 BAND
ALABASTER $1700
ALABASTER+MAROON $2500
MAROON+ALABASTER $2500

SENTINAL 195ULTA CA1940
'WRAP-AROUND GRILLE'
CATALIN, 5 TUBES, 1 BAND
ALABASTER+TORTOISE $3500

SENTINAL 284 CA1946
'WAVE GRILLE'
CATALIN, 5 TUBES, 1 BAND
ALABASTER $1800
BLUE+ALABASTER $3000
RED+ALABASTER $2500

SETCHELL-CARLSON 416 CA1946
'FROG EYES'
STYRENE, 5 TUBES, 1 BAND
BROWN+IVORY $125, IVORY $150
BLUE+IVORY $400, RED+IVORY $275

SETCHELL-CARLSON 427 CA1946
'BIG FROG EYES'
STYRENE, 5 TUBES, 1 BAND
BROWN+IVORY $125, IVORY $150
BLUE+IVORY $375, RED+IVORY $250

SILVER 5E CA1939
'TINY TIM'
BAKELITE, 5 TUBES, 1 BAND
BLACK $100, BROWN OR PAINTED $75

SILVER 515-5A CA1939
BAKELITE, 5 TUBES, 1 BAND
BROWN OR PAINTED $150

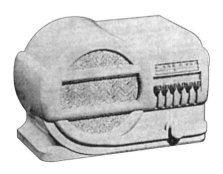

SILVER 516-C CA1939
5 TUBES, 1 BAND
BROWN OR PAINTED BAKELITE $60
IVORY PLASKON $100

SILVER 519 CA1940
BAKELITE, 5 TUBES, 1 BAND
BROWN OR PAINTED $350

SILVER 635 CA1940
BAKELITE, 6 TUBES, 1 BAND
BROWN OR PAINTED $125

SILVER T569 CA1940
5 TUBES, 1 BAND
BROWN OR PAINTED BAKELITE $70
IVORY PLASKON $110

SILVER B666 CA1940
6 TUBES, 1 BAND
BROWN OR PAINTED BAKELITE $175
IVORY PLASKON $225

SILVER B667P CA1940
6 TUBES, 1 BAND
BROWN OR PAINTED BAKELITE $225
IVORY PLASKON $275

SILVER TS105 CA1940
5 TUBES, 1 BAND
BAKELITE: BROWN $45, BLACK $55
IVORY PLASKON $90

SILVERTONE 4 CA1960
STYRENE, 5 TUBES, 1 BAND
BROWN $15, IVORY $20
GREEN $40, RED $60

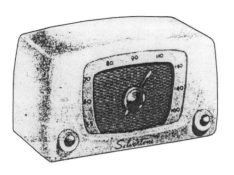

SILVERTONE 6 CA1951
BAKELITE, 5 TUBES, 1 BAND
BROWN OR PAINTED $40

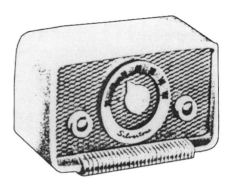

SILVERTONE 13 CA1951
BAKELITE, 5 TUNES, 1 BAND
BROWN OR PAINTED $40

SILVERTONE 7-10,19-22 CA1960
STYRENE, 5 TUBES, 1 BAND
BROWN $15, IVORY $20
BLUE $50, RED $60, GREEN $50

SILVERTONE 11,25 CA1960
11BROWN, 12IVORY, 13BLUE
STYRENE, 6 TUBES, 1 BAND
BROWN $20, IVORY $25
BLUE $50

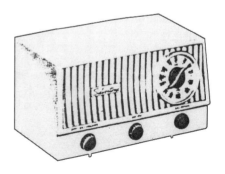

SILVERTONE 15 CA1950
BAKELITE, 5 TUBES, 1 BAND
BROWN OR PAINTED $20

SILVERTONE 27 CA1952
BAKELITE, 5 TUBES, 1 BAND
BROWN OR PAINTED $20

SILVERTONE 35,1034 CA1960
STYRENE, 5 TUBES, 1 BAND
BROWN $15, IVORY $20
GREEN $45, PINK $60

SILVERTONE 39 CA1960
STYRENE, 5 TUBES, 1 BAND
BROWN $20, IVORY $25, BLUE $60

SILVERTONE 47 CA1959
STYRENE TRANSISTOR
GRAY $25, IVORY $25
GREEN $45, RED $60

SILVERTONE 215 CA1951
STYRENE, 5 TUBES, 1 BAND
IVORY $45, BLACK $40
GREEN $50, MAROON $50

SILVERTONE 1036 CA1959
STYRENE, 5 TUBES, 1 BAND
IVORY $15, TAN $20

SILVERTONE 2004 CA1954
STYRENE, 5 TUBES, 1 BAND
IVORY $20, BLACK $20
GRAY $25

SILVERTONE 2013 CA1954
STYRENE, 5 TUBES, 1 BAND
IVORY $15, TAN $20
GREEN $30

SILVERTONE 2015 CA1954
BAKELITE, 5 TUBES, 1 BAND
BROWN OR PAINTED $15

SILVERTONE 2074 CA1960
STYRENE, 5 TUBES, 1 BAND
IVORY $75, TAN $70
PINK $100, GREEN $90

SILVERTONE 2210 CA1953
STYRENE, 4 TUBES, 1 BAND
IVORY $65, BLACK $60
MAROON $75

SILVERTONE 3002 CA1954
STYRENE, 5 TUBES, 1 BAND
IVORY, BLACK $25

SILVERTONE 3005 CA1954
STYRENE, 5 TUBES, 1 BAND
IVORY, BLACK $15

SILVERTONE 3007 CA1954
STYRENE, 5 TUBES, 1 BAND
IVORY, BLACK $25

SILVERTONE 3011,7000 CA1941
'LEFT-HANDED DIAL'
5 TUBES, 1 BAND
BROWN OR PAINTED BAKELITE $100
PLASKON: IVORY $125, BEETLE $250

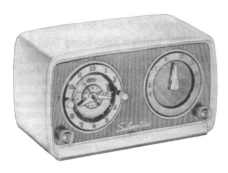

SILVERTONE 3026 CA1954
STYRENE, 5 TUBES, 1 BAND
IVORY, BLACK $15

SILVERTONE 3051,6403 CA1938
5 TUBES, 1 BAND
BAKELITE: BROWN OR PAINTED $75, BLACK $125
PLASKON: IVORY $175, BEETLE $400

3061 NOTE: TENITE GRILL AND KNOBS NEARLY ALWAYS
BADLY WARPED. SUBTRACT 25-50% OF VALUE

SILVERTONE 3061 CA1940
6 TUBES, 1 BAND
BROWN OR PAINTED BAKELITE+TAN TENITE $125
PAINTED IVORY+BLUE TENITE $150
BEETLE PLASKON+TAN TENITE $300
BEETLE PLASKON+BLUE TENITE $350

SILVERTONE 3541 CA1939
4 TUBES, 1 BAND
BROWN OR PAINTED BAKELITE $90
RED PLASKON $400

SILVERTONE 3215 CA1953
STYRENE, 4 TUBES, 1 BAND
GREY $20
RED $60, GREEN $45

SILVERTONE 4025 CA1954
STYRENE, 6 TUBES, 1 BAND
BROWN $20, IVORY $25

4500: FIRST SILVERTONE BAKELITE RADIO: MARKETED
FOR THE 1936 PRESIDENTIAL ELECTION NEWS

SILVERTONE 4414,4500 CA1936
'ELECTION'
5 TUBES, 1 BAND
BAKELITE: BROWN $75, BLACK $100
PLASKON: IVORY $175, PINK $1,500
LAVENDER $2000

SILVERTONE 6102 CA1936
6 TUBES, 1 BAND
BLACK BAKELITE $125
IVORY PLASKON $200

SILVERTONE 3351,7004 CA1939
'CANDYCANE'
4-5 TUBES, 1 BAND
BROWN OR PAINTED BAKELITE $80
BEETLE PLASKON $250

SILVERTONE 6009 CA1946
BAKELITE, 5 TUBES, 1 BAND
BROWN OR PAINTED $20

SILVERTONE 6016 CA1947
BAKELITE, 5 TUBES, 1 BAND
BROWN OR PAINTED $25

SILVERTONE 6110 CA1938
'ROCKET'
KARSTADT DESIGN
5 TUBES, 1 BAND
BAKELITE: BROWN $1700, BLACK $2000
IVORY PLASKON $2,500
6110 - IVORY $2500

SILVERTONE 6165 CA1939
'SILVERTONE JUNIOR'
4 TUBES, 1 BAND
BAKELITE: BROWN $110, BLACK $125
PLASKON: IVORY $175, RED $450

SILVERTONE 6177 CA1939
'SILVERTONE BULLET'
5 TUBES, 1 BAND
BAKELITE: BROWN $200, BLACK $250, 6178
IVORY PLASKON $350

SILVERTONE 6400 CA1939
BAKELITE, 4 TUBES, 1 BAND
BROWN OR PAINTED IVORY $135
BLACK $175

SILVERTONE 6318 CA1939
'UPSIDE-DOWN CHASSIS'
BAKELITE, 6 TUBES, 1 BAND
BROWN OR PAINTED IVORY $125, BLACK $150

SILVERTONE 6020 CA1956
STYRENE, 5 TUBES, 1 BAND
BROWN $15, IVORY $20

SILVERTONE 6201 CA1946
BAKELITE, 4 TUBES, 1 BAND, DC
BROWN OR PAINTED IVORY $20

SILVERTONE 7001 CA1957
STYRENE, 5 TUBES, 1 BAND
BLACK $40, IVORY $30

SILVERTONE 7003 CA1957
STYRENE, 5 TUBES, 1 BAND
BROWN $15, IVORY $20

SILVERTONE 7006 CA1957
STYRENE
STYRENE, 5 TUBES, 1 BAND
BLACK $25, IVORY $20

SILVERTONE 7013 CA1957
STYRENE, 5 TUBES, 1 BAND
BLACK $25, IVORY $20
GREEN $35, RED $40

SILVERTONE 7016 CA1942
BAKELITE, 6 TUBES, 2 BANDS
BROWN OR PAINTED $20

SILVERTONE 7021 CA1947
BAKELITE, 5 TUBES, 1 BAND
BROWN OR PAINTED $75

SILVERTONE 8005 CA1949
BAKELITE, 5 TUBES, 1 BAND
BLACK $30, METALLIC BLUE $40

SILVERTONE 8020 CA1949
BAKELITE, 8 TUBES, AM+FM
BLACK $35, METALLIC BLUE $45

SILVERTONE 8000 CA1949
'UPSIDE-DOWN CHASSIS'
BAKELITE, 4 TUBES, 1 BAND
BROWN OR PAINTED $60

SILVERTONE 8010 CA1948
BAKELITE, 5 TUBES, 1 BAND
BLACK $60, PAINTED IVORY $50

SILVERTONE 7020 CA1957
STYRENE, 5 TUBES, 1 BAND
$25

SILVERTONE 8017 CA1958
STYRENE
$15

SILVERTONE 8022 CA1949
BAKELITE, 7 TUBES, AM+FM
$20

SILVERTONE 7204 CA1957
STYRENE, 7 TUBES, AM+FM
$15

SILVERTONE 8217 CA1959
STYRENE, 4 TUBES, 1 BAND
TAN+IVORY $75

SILVERTONE 9000 CA1951
BAKELITE, 5 TUBES, 1 BAND
BROWN OR PAINTED $35, BLACK $40

SILVERTONE 9004 CA1958
STYRENE
1873 $15

SILVERTONE 9018 CA1957
'METEOR'
STYRENE, 4 TUBES, 1 BAND
$25

SILVERTONE 9021 CA1958
STYRENE, 5 TUBES, 1 BAND
$15

SILVERTONE 9260 CA1949
STYRENE, 4 TUBES, 1 BAND
IVORY $80

NOTE: CORONET PRODUCTION WAS LIMITED BECAUSE
OF CABINET FRAGILITY. NEAR PERFECT EXAMPLES ARE
EXTREMELY RARE.

SILVERTONE 'CORONET' CA1937
6 TUBES, 1 BAND
BLACK BAKELITE $1700
IVORY PLASKON $2200

SILVERTONE 'WEDGE' CA1960
STYRENE, TRANSISTOR, 1 BAND
$75

SONIC 'PEE WEE' CA1956
STYRENE, 4 TUBES, 1 BAND
IVORY $90, AQUA $125, PINK $115

SONORA 11 CA1949
'PETER PAN'
BAKELITE, 5 TUBES, 1 BAND
BAKELITE: BROWN OR PAINTED $45

SONORA 22 CA1939
BAKELITE: BROWN OR PAINTED $75, BLACK $90
IVORY PLASKON $125
IVORY PLASKON+BLACK BAKELITE $200

SONORA 62 CA1940
5 TUBES, 1 BAND
BAKELITE: BROWN OR PAINTED $75, BLACK $90
IVORY PLASKON $125

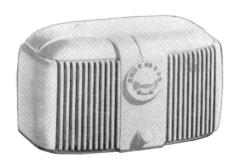

SONORA 48 CA1940
BAKELITE, 5 TUBES, 1 BAND
BAKELITE: BROWN OR PAINTED $120

SONORA 49 CA1939
5 TUBES, 1 BAND
BROWN OR PAINTED BAKELITE $250
BLACK BAKELITE $300
BEETLE PLASKON $1200

SONORA 100 CA1949
BAKELITE, 5 TUBES, 1 BAND
BAKELITE: BROWN OR PAINTED $20

SONORA 101 CA1939
'JUBILEE'
BAKELITE, 4 TUBES, 1 BAND
BROWN OR PAINTED $125

SONORA 106 CA1939
'METRO'
BAKELITE, 4 TUBES, 1 BAND
BROWN OR PAINTED $110

SONORA 108 CA1940
BAKELITE, 4 TUBES, 1 BAND
BROWN OR PAINTED $60

SONORA 105 CA1939
'COSMO'
BAKELITE, 5 TUBES, 1 BAND
BROWN OR PAINTED $60

SONORA LM 'STRATOLINER' CA1942
BAKELITE, 5 TUBES, 1 BAND, AC-DC
BROWN OR PAINTED $25

SONORA KT CA1941
'CAMEO'
BAKELITE, 5 TUBES, 1 BAND
BROWN OR PAINTED $20

SONORA 138 CA1941
'CORONET'
CATALIN, 5 TUBES, 1 BAND
ALABASTER+GREEN $1800
ALABASTER+RED $1500

SONORA 222 CA1946
BAKELITE, 5 TUBES, 1 BAND
BROWN OR PAINTED $75

SONORA 240 CA1948
BAKELITE, 8 TUBES, AM+FM
BROWN OR PAINTED $150

SONORA 252 CA1941
PAINTED BAKELITE, 4 TUBES, 1 BAND, DC
IVORY $100, AQUA+MAROON $150
TAN+AQUA $135, MAROON+TAN $125

SONORA LQ 'CLIPPER' CA1942
5 TUBES, 1 BAND, AC-DC
BROWN OR PAINTED $30

SPARTON 100 CA1948
BAKELITE, 5 TUBES, 1 BAND
BROWN OR PAINTED $30
BLACK $40

SPARTON 'EASY-GOER' CA1954
STYRENE, 5 TUBES, 1 BAND
BLACK $100, WHITE $100
GREEN $175, RED $200

SPARTON 132 CA1950
'FOOTBALL'
STYRENE, 5 TUBES, 1 BAND
BLACK $110, WHITE $110
GREEN $125, MAROON $125

SPARTON 315C CA1952
'FOOTBALL'
STYRENE, 5 TUBES, 1 BAND
BLACK $120, WHITE $110
GREEN $140, MAROON $140

SPARTON 'MORNING STAR' CA1954
STYRENE, 5 TUBES, 1 BAND
BLACK $110, GREEN $135
IVORY $110, RED $140

SPARTON 'TABLE TOPPER' CA1954
STYRENE, 5 TUBES, 1 BAND
BLACK $100, GREEN $125
IVORY $100, RED $130

SPARTON 5G1-K CA1958
STYRENE, 5 TUBES, 1 BAND
IVORY $35, BLACK $45
RED $60, GREEN $60

SPARTON CANADA 5048L CA1948
BAKELITE, 5 TUBES, 1 BAND
$50

SPARTON CANADA CA1939
'SPLIT GRILLE'
BAKELITE+TENITE, 5 TUBES, 1 BAND
$500

SPARTON CANADA CA1940
'SPLIT GRILLE'
BAKELITE+TENITE, 5 TUBES, 1 BAND
$350

STANDARD CA1949
STYRENE, 5 TUBES, 1 BAND
IVORY $60, BLACK $65
YELLOW $125, PINK $125, LAVENDER $200

STEWART-WARNER R206-FA CA1941
BAKELITE, 6 TUBES, 2 BANDS
$75

SPARTON 500 CA1939
'CLOISONNE'
CATALIN CABINET+COPPER ENAMEL FACE
YELLOW CABINET, YELLOW FACE $4000
YELLOW CABINET, RED FACE $5000
YELLOW CABINET, BLUE FACE $5000

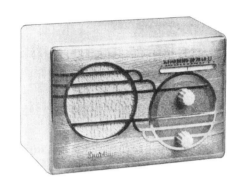

SPARTON 608B CA1939
'POLO'
6 TUBES, 1 BAND
POLO PLAYER EMBOSSED ON TOP
BROWN BAKELITE $500
BLACK BAKELITE $750
IVORY PLASKON $1200
RED PLASKON $2500

STEWART-WARNER
9014E CA1942
CATALIN, 5 TUBES, 1 BAND
DARK GREEN+YELLOW $1500

STEWART-WARNER 5R3 CA1941
'CAMPUS'
5 TUBES, 1 BAND
BROWN BAKELITE $125
IVORY PLASKON $200

STEWART-WARNER 7-511,3-SK3 CA1939
'CAMPUS'
5 TUBES, 1 BAND
BROWN BAKELITE $150
IVORY PLASKON $225

STEWART-WARNER 7-5B,97-562 CA1939
'SENIOR VARSITY'
BAKELITE, 5 TUBES, 1 BAND
BROWN OR PAINTED FINISH $350
NOTE: MARKETED IN NUMEROUS PAINTED COLLEGE
TEAM COLORS

STEWART-WARNER A65 CA1938
'AIRPAL'
BAKELITE, 3 TUBES, 1 BAND
BROWN OR PAINTED IVORY $200

STEWART-WARNER A51-T3 CA1949
'AIR PAL'
BAKELITE, 4 TUBES, 1 BAND
BROWN OR PAINTED $150

STEWART-WARNER B51-T CA1940
'AIR PAL'
BAKELITE, 4 TUBES, 1 BAND
BROWN OR PAINTED $125

STEWART-WARNER 205A CA1942
BAKELITE, 5 TUBES, 1 BAND
BROWN OR PAINTED $20

STEWART-WARNER 206D CA1942
BAKELITE, 6 TUBES, 2 BANDS
BROWN OR PAINTED $25

STEWART-WARNER 9151A CA1948
5 TUBES, 1 BAND
BROWN BAKELITE+IVORY PLASKON
$30

STEWART-WARNER 9152A CA1948
BAKELITE, 5 TUBES, 1 BAND
$20

STEWART-WARNER A72T1 CA1948
'STREAMLINER'
BAKELITE, 6 TUBES, 1 BAND
BROWN OR PAINTED $50
BLACK $70

STEWART-WARNER C51T1 CA1950
BAKELITE, 5 TUBES, 1 BAND
BROWN OR PAINTED $40

STEWART-WARNER 9162 CA1952
2-TONE PAINTED BAKELITE
$50

STEWART-WARNER 9182 CA1954
2-TONE PAINTED BAKELITE
$60

**STEWART-WARNER CANADA
9181 CA1956**
STYRENE, 5 TUBES, 1 BAND
$40

**STEWART-WARNER CANADA
9187 CA1956**
STYRENE, 5 TUBES, 1 BAND
$60

**STROMBERG-CARLSON
600H CA1941**
BAKELITE, 6 TUBES, 1 BAND
$75

**STROMBERG-CARLSON
761H,900H CA1941**
BAKELITE, 6 TUBES, 1 BAND
$60

STROMBERG-CARLSON
1204-H CA1948
BAKELITE, 8 TUBES, AM-FM
$75

STROMBERG-CARLSON
1500H CA1951
BAKELITE, 5 TUBES, 1 BAND
BROWN BAKELITE $60
MAROON BAKELITE $150

STROMBERG-CARLSON
C1 CA1951
BAKELITE, 5 TUBES, 1 BAND,
$30

STROMBERG-CARLSON
C3 CA1955
BAKELITE, 5 TUBES, 1 BAND,
$25

STROMBERG-CARLSON CANADA
1051 CA1939
BAKELITE, 5 TUBES, 1 BAND
BROWN OR PAINTED $175

SUPERHET 64183 CA1940
BAKELITE, 5 TUBES, 1 BAND
BROWN OR PAINTED $150

SUPERHET 64185 CA1940
BAKELITE, 6 TUBES, 2 BANDS, AC-DC
BROWN OR PAINTED $50

SUPERHET 64187 CA1940
BAKELITE, 6 TUBES, 2 BANDS, AC-DC
BROWN OR PAINTED $50

SYLVANIA 5C10E CA1957
'TEMPOTIMER'
STYRENE, 5 TUBES, 1 BAND
TAN $40, BLUE $60

SYLVANIA 5T10E CA1960
'BOLERO'
STYRENE, 5 TUBES, 1 BAND
TAN $25, BLUE $50

SYLVANIA 5C12E CA1957
'NITELITER'
STYRENE, 5 TUBES, 1 BAND
PINK $125, AQUA $135, TAN $75

SYLVANIA 5T12E CA1959
'PARK AVENUE'
STYRENE, 5 TUBES, 1 BAND
PINK $125, AQUA $135, TAN $75

SYLVANIA 5C13E CA1957
'SKYLITER'
STYRENE, 5 TUBES, 1 BAND,
PINK $65, BLUE $60, TAN $30

SYLVANIA 8F15E CA1960
'RECITAL'
STYRENE, TRANSISTOR, AMFM
$35

SYLVANIA 5T13E CA1959
'TWIN TONE'
STYRENE, 5 TUBES, 1 BAND
PINK $60, TAN $35, BLUE $65

SYLVANIA 5T14E CA1959
'MUSIC MASTER'
STYRENE, 5 TUBES, 1 BAND
PINK $60, TAN $35, BLUE $65

SYLVANIA 8F16E CA1961
'INTERLUDE'
STYRENE, 8 TUBES, AM-FM
$50

SYLVANIA 519 CA1955
STYRENE, 5 TUBES, 1 BAND
TAN $35, BLACK $40
GREEN $60, RED $75

SYLVANIA 543 CA1955
STYRENE, 5 TUBES, 1 BAND
$30

SYLVANIA 548 CA1955
STYRENE, 5 TUBES, 1 BAND
TAN $20, BLACK $25
GREEN $40, RED $50

SYLVANIA 563B CA1953
STYRENE, 5 TUBES, 1 BAND
TAN $25, BLACK $25
GREEN $50, RED $75

SYLVANIA 5184 CA1955
STYRENE, 5 TUBES, 1 BAND
IVORY $20, BLACK $20
GREEN $40, RED $50

SYLVANIA 598 CA1955
STYRENE, 5 TUBES, 1 BAND
TAN $25, BLACK $25
GREEN $45, RED $65

SYLVANIA 614 CA1955
STYRENE, 5 TUBES, 1 BAND
TAN $20, BLACK $25
GREEN $40, RED $60

SYLVANIA 1107E CA1959
'SYMPHOTONE'
STYRENE, 5 TUBES, 1 BAND
BLACK $30

SYLVANIA 2108E CA1959
'SWINGTIMER'
STYRENE, 5 TUBES, 1 BAND
BLACK $30

SYLVANIA 619 CA1960
STYRENE, 5 TUBES, 1 BAND
BLACK $40, WHITE, $40
TAN $40, PINK $60

SYLVANIA 5151 CA1955
STYRENE, 5 TUBES, 1 BAND
IVORY $25, BLACK $30
GREEN $45, RED $60

SYLVANIA 'CATALINA' CA1953
STYRENE, 5 TUBES, 1 BAND, AC-DC
TAN $30, BLACK $40
GREEN $50, RED $65

TELETONE 109 CA1947
BAKELITE, 5 TUBES, 1 BAND
$40

TELETONE 109W CA1947
BAKELITE, 5 TUBES, 1 BAND
$30

TELETONE 135 CA1947
STYRENE, 5 TUBES, 1 BAND
BLACK $35, IVORY $45

TELETONE 156 CA1948
STYRENE, 5 TUBES, 1 BAND
MARBELED TAN $110
BLACK $35, IVORY $40

TELETONE 157 CA1948
STYRENE, 5 TUBES, 1 BAND
BLACK $35, IVORY $40

TELETONE 158 CA1949
BAKELITE, 5 TUBES, 1 BAND
2081 $30

TELETONE 165 CA1949
STYRENE, 5 TUBES, 1 BAND
MARBELED BROWN $125
BLACK $35, IVORY $40

TELETONE 184 CA1949
STYRENE, 5 TUBES, 1 BAND
BLACK $25, IVORY $25

TELETONE 190 CA1949
STYRENE, 5 TUBES, 1 BAND
BLACK $30, IVORY $35
MARBELED TAN $75

TELETONE 228 CA1951
STYRENE, 5 TUBES, 1 BAND
BLACK $45, TAN $40
RED $65

TELETONE 230 CA1951
STYRENE, 5 TUBES, 1 BAND
BLACK $40, IVORY $45

TELETONE TR70 CA1950
STYRENE, 5 TUBES, 1 BAND
BROWN $30 IVORY $45
TAN $40

TELETONE TR155 CA1958
STYRENE, 4 TUBES, 1 BAND
IVORY $90, AQUA $125, PINK $115

TELECHRON 8H67 CA1948
BAKELITE: BROWN OR PAINTED $30
MARBELED PLASKON (PINK+BLUE+GRAY)
$350

TINY TIM 526-4H CA1940
BAKELITE, 4 TUBES, 1 BAND
BROWN OR PAINTED $75

TINY TIM PEE WEE CA1939
BAKELITE, 4 TUBES, 1 BAND
BROWN OR PAINTED $75

TRAVLER 30 CA1951
STYRENE, 6 TUBES, 1 BAND
IVORY+BLACK OR BROWN $50

TRAVLER 36 CA1951
BAKELITE, 6 TUBES, 1 BAND
BROWN OR PAINTED $35

TRAVLER 55C42 CA1955
STYRENE, 5 TUBES, 1 BAND
BLACK $25, IVORY $30

TRAVLER 66 CA1951
BAKELITE, 7 TUBES, FM
$25

TRAVLER 5025 CA1947
BAKELITE, 5 TUBES, 1 BAND
$20

TRAVLER 5051 CA1948
BAKELITE, 5 TUBES, 1 BAND
$30

TRAVLER 5055 CA1948
4 TUBES, 1 BAND
BAKELITE WITH TENITE GRILLE $35

TRAVLER 5060 CA1950
BAKELITE, 5 TUBES, 1 BAND
$45

TRAVLER 5061 CA1950
BAKELITE, 5 TUBES, 1 BAND
$30

TRAVLER T-2O3 CA1959
5 TUBES, 1 BAND
STYRENE WITH OAINTED GRILLE
BLACK+YELLOW $135
IVORY+PINK $150, IVORY+BLUE $150

TROUBADOR 2531 CA1947
BAKELITE, 5 TUBES, 1 BAND
BROWN OR PAINTED $45

TROUBADOR 2533 CA1947
'BULLET'
BAKELITE, 5 TUBES, 1 BAND
BROWN OR PAINTED $150

TROUBADOR 2561 CA1947
BAKELITE, 5 TUBES, 1 BAND
$2O

TRUETONE 9O52 CA1947
4 TUBES, 1 BAND
BROWN BAKELITE $30, BLACK BAKELITE $40
IVORY PLASKON $6O

TRUETONE D73O CA1938
5 TUBES, 1 BAND
BROWN BAKELITE $45, BLACK BAKELITE $60
IVORY PLASKON $100

TRUETONE D636 CA1938
BAKELITE, 5 TUBES, 1 BAND
BROWN OR PAINTED $125

TRUETONE D731 CA1938
BAKELITE, 5 TUBES, 1 BAND
BROWN OR PAINTED $125

TRUETONE THREE-WAY CA1938
6 TUBES, 1 BAND
BLACK BAKELITE+CHROME $275
IVORY PLASKON+BRASS $350

TRUETONE D909 CA1939
'JUNIOR'
4 TUBES, 1 BAND
BAKELITE: BROWN $100
PLASKON: IVORY $175, RED $600

TRUETONE D915 CA1939
'STRATOSCOPE'
5 TUBES, 1 BAND
BROWN BAKELITE $175
PLASKON IVORY: $225, BEETLE $400

TRUETONE D1011,D2615 CA1946
BAKELITE, 5 TUBES, 1 BAND
BROWN OR PAINTED $85

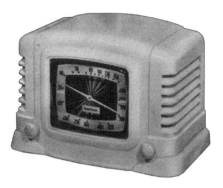

TRUETONE D1124,D1015,2610 CA1947
'GEM'
BAKELITE, 5 TUBES, 1 BAND
BROWN OR PAINTED $125

TRUETONE D1019 CA1942
BAKELITE, 5 TUBES, 1 BAND
BROWN OR PAINTED $15

TRUETONE D1118 CA1942
BAKELITE, 7 TUBES, 2 BANDS
BROWN OR PAINTED $20

TRUETONE D2018 CA1950
'BOOMERANG'
BAKELITE, 5 TUBES, 1 BAND
BROWN OR PAINTED $275

TRUETONE D2026 CA1952
8 TUBES, AM-FM
BROWN OR PAINTED $30

TRUETONE D2103 CA1952
BAKELITE, 5 TUBES, 1 BAND
BROWN OR PAINTED $30

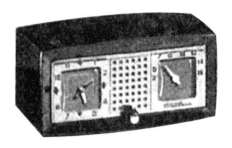

TRUETONE D2216 CA1952
BAKELITE, 5 TUBES, 1 BAND,
$20

TRUETONE D2237 CA1954
BAKELITE, 6 TUBES, 1 BAND
BROWN OR PAINTED $40

TRUETONE D2389 CA1953
BAKELITE, 5 TUBES, 1 BAND
BROWN OR PAINTED $30

TRUETONE D2410 CA1954
STYRENE, 5 TUBES, 1 BAND
IVORY $20, TAN $20
RED $65, GREEN $50

TRUETONE D2418 CA1954
STYRENE, 4 TUBES, 1 BAND
BLACK $25, RED $50
IVORY $20

TRUETONE D2582 CA1954
STYRENE, 5 TUBES, 1 BAND
IVORY $25, TAN $20
RED $75

TRUETONE D2613 CA1947
BAKELITE, 5 TUBES, 1 BAND
BROWN OR PAINTED $25

TRUETONE D2616A CA1947
BAKELITE, 6 TUBES, 1 BAND
BROWN OR PAINTED $150

TRUETONE D2637 CA1954
4 TUBES, 1 BAND
STYRENE WITH PAINTED TRIM
BLACK+PINK $60

TRUETONE D2684-5 CA1954
BAKELITE, 5 TUBES, 1 BAND
BROWN OR PAINTED $40

TRUETONE D2693 CA1948
BAKELITE, 5 TUBES, 1 BAND
BROWN OR PAINTED $25

TRUETONE D2718 CA1948
BAKELITE, 5 TUBES, 1 BAND
BROWN OR PAINTED $40

TRUETONE D2762 CA1948
BAKELITE, 5 TUBES, 1 BAND
BROWN OR PAINTED $20

TRUETONE D2781 CA1956
STYRENE, 5 TUBES, 1 BAND
IVORY $50, BLACK $50
RED $90

TRUETONE D3809 CA1946
STYRENE, 4 TUBES, 1 BAND, DC
MARBELED TAN $110
BLACK $35, IVORY $40

TRUETONE DC2036 CA1960
STYRENE, 5 TUBES, 1 BAND
BLACK $60, IVORY $60
RED $100, PINK $90, AQUA $90

TRUETONE DC2170 CA1960
STYRENE, 4 TUBES, 1 BAND
BLACK $15, IVORY $15

TRUETONE DC2371,DC2362 CA1961
STYRENE, 5 TUBES, 1 BAND
2634 $30

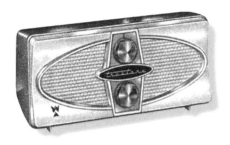

TRUETONE DC2380 CA1961
STYRENE, 5 TUBES, 1 BAND
$50

VOGUE 'STREAMLINE' CA1939
5 TUBES, 1 BAND
BROWN BAKELITE $125
IVORY PLASKON $200

WARWICK O-76 CA1948
BAKELITE, 5 TUBES, 1 BAND
$150

WELLS-GARDNER 5D2 CA1937
BAKELITE, 5 TUBES, 1 BAND
BROWN OR PAINTED $125

WELLS-GARDNER 7D14 CA1947
BAKELITE, 7 TUBES, 2 BANDS
BROWN OR PAINTED $60

WESTERN 59-1744 CA1941
'AIR PATROL'
5 TUBES, 2 BANDS
BROWN BAKELITE $60, IVORY PLASKON $125

WESTINGHOUSE 327-T6 CA1951
5 TUBES, 1 BAND
BAKELITE WITH STYRENE GRILLE $40

WESTINGHOUSE 345-T5 CA1951
BAKELITE, 5 TUBES, 1 BAND
$25

WESTINGHOUSE 356-T5 CA1951
PAINTED BAKELITE, 5 TUBES, 1 BAND
BROWN $50, IVORY $60, TAN $60
RED $75, GREEN $65

WESTINGHOUSE 434T5 CA1957
STYRENE, 5 TUBES, 1 BANDS
BLACK, IVORY $50, TAN $55
GRAY $60, GREEN $90 RED $110

WESTINGHOUSE 486T5 CA1957
STYRENE, 5 TUBES, 1 BANDS
BLACK, IVORY $30
GRAY $40, RED $60

WESTINGHOUSE 501T5,626T5 CA1957
STYRENE, 5 TUBES, 1 BAND
IVORY, BLACK $40, TAN $50, RED $90
GREEN $80, YELLOE $90, AQUA $85
GRAY+PLAID $75

WESTINGHOUSE 520P4 CA1955
STYRENE, 4 TUBES, 1 BAND
MAROON $50, TAN $40,
RED $90, BLACK $40

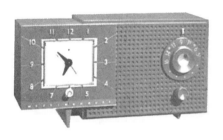

WESTINGHOUSE 536T6 CA1957
STYRENE, 6 TUBES, 1 BAND
BLACK, IVORY $50, TAN $55
GRAY $60, GREEN $90 RED $110

WESTINGHOUSE 538T4 CA1955
STYRENE, 4 TUBES, 1 BAND
2663 BLACK $75,
IVORY $60, RED $100

WESTINGHOUSE 544T5,570T4 CA1957
STYRENE, 5 TUBES, 1 BAND
GRAY $50, BROWN $40, IVORY $45
BLACK $50, PINK $90

WESTINGHOUSE 547T5 CA1957
STYRENE, 5 TUBES, 1 BAND
BLACK $45, PINK $90
RED $120, GREEN $80

WESTINGHOUSE 598P4 CA1957
STYRENE, 4 TUBES, 1 BAND
GREEN $75, WHITE-TAN $65
GRAY-BLACK $60

WESTINGHOUSE 562P4 CA1957
STYRENE, 4 TUBES, 1 BAND
TAN-BROWN $45, WHITE-TAN $45
GRAY-BLACK $50

WESTINGHOUSE 574T4,629T4 CA1957
STYRENE, 4 TUBES, 1 BAND
BLACK $60, IVORY $50, PINK $75
RED $125, LT GREEN $80, LT BLUE $75

WESTINGHOUSE 580T5 CA1957
STYRENE, 4 TUBES, 1 BAND
BROWN $45, IVORY $50
RED $135

WESTINGHOUSE 621PX CA1957
STYRENE, 6 TUBES, 1 BAND
GRAY $80, YELLOW $110

WESTINGHOUSE 632T5 CA1957
STYRENE, 5 TUBES, 1 BAND
TAN $20, AQUA $30

WESTINGHOUSE 640T5 CA1957
STYRENE, 5 TUBES, 1 BAND
BROWN $15, AQUA $35
IVORY $20, RED $50

WESTINGHOUSE H320T5 CA1950
STYRENE, 5 TUBES, 1 BAND
BROWN $45, IVORY $50
GREEN $75, RED $90

WESTINGHOUSE H125 CA1946
'LITTLE JEWEL'
'REFRIGERATOR'
PAINTED BAKELITE, 5 TUBES, 1 BAND
IVORY $125
LT GREEN $150
TEAL BLUE $150

WESTINGHOUSE H204 CA1948
PAINTED BAKELITE, 8 TUBES, AM-FM
BROWN $40, IVORY $50
GREEN $60

WESTINGHOUSE H398T5 CA1955
'REFRIGERATOR'
STYRENE, 5 TUBES, 1 BAND,
BROWN $50,
IVORY $75
RED $125

WESTINGHOUSE H342-P5 CA1951
STYRENE, 5 TUBES, 1 BAND
BLACK+RED
$350

WESTINGHOUSE H418-T5 CA1954
STYRENE, 5 TUBES, 1 BAND
BROWN $50, IVORY $75
RED $150

WESTINGHOUSE H404-T5 CA1953
STYRENE, 5 TUBES, 1 BAND
BROWN $20, IVORY $25
RED $50

**WESTINGHOUSE
452T5,524T4,648T4 CA1958**
STYRENE, 5 TUBES, 1 BAND
BROWN $20, IVORY $25, RED $125
GREEN $75, BLUE $85

WESTINGHOUSE 461P4 CA1954
STYRENE 4 TUBES, 1 BAND
IVORY $30, RED $75, GREEN $50
MARBLED BROWN $75

WESTINGHOUSE H504P4 CA1957
STYRENE, 4 TUBES, 1 BAND
MAROON $65, BLACK $50
RED $125, GREEN $75

WESTINGHOUSE WR12 CA1942
BAKELITE, 5 TUBES, 1 BAND
$20

WESTINGHOUSE WR120 CA1938
BAKELITE, 6 TUBES, 1 BAND
$60

WESTINGHOUSE WR166 CA1938
5 TUBES, 1 BAND
BROWN BAKELITE $150
IVORY PLASKON $300

WESTINGHOUSE WR173 CA1940
5 TUBES, 1 BAND
BROWN BAKELITE $75
IVORY PLASKON $125

WESTINGHOUSE WR175 CA1939
BAKELITE, 5 TUBES, 1 BAND
BROWN OR PAINTED $40

**WESTINGHOUSE CANADA
501M CA1950**
PLASKON, 4 TUBES, 1 BAND
IVORY $50, LT BLUE $125

WESTINGHOUSE CANADA
576 CA1940
BAKELITE, 5 TUBES, 1 BAND
BROWN OR PAINTED $20

WESTINGHOUSE CANADA
604 CA1949
BAKELITE, 6 TUBES, 3 BANDS
BROWN OR PAINTED $25

WESTINGHOUSE CANADA
H310-T5 CA1950
STYRENE, 5 TUBES, 1 BAND
IVORY $40, GREEN $60, RED $90

WESTINGHOUSE CANADA
X2395-11 CA1958
STYRENE, 5 TUBES, 1 BAND
BROWN $20, IVORY $25, RED $75

WILCOX-GAY A51 CA1938
'LIL CHAMP'
4 TUBES, 1 BAND
BROWN BAKELITE $225
PLASKON: IVORY $350, LT GREEN $650

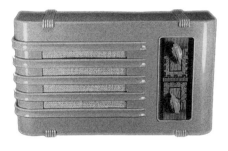

WILCOX-GAY A53 CA1938
'THIN MAN'
5 TUBES, 1 BAND
BROWN BAKELITE $200
PLASKON: IVORY $350, LT GREEN $800

ZENITH 11 CA1946
BAKELITE, 5 TUBES, 1 BAND
BROWN OR PAINTED $20

ZENITH 14 CA1946
BAKELITE, 5 TUBES, 1 BAND
BROWN OR PAINTED $50

ZENITH 15 CA1946
6 TUBES, 1 BAND
BROWN OR PAINTED BAKELITE $40
MAROON STYRENE $125

ZENITH 23 CA1946
BAKELITE, 5 TUBES, 1 BAND
BROWN OR PAINTED $35

ZENITH 311 CA1939
'WAVEMAGNET'
BAKELITE, 5 TUBES, 2 BANDS
BROWN OR PAINTED $250, BLACK $300

ZENITH 510, 516 CA1941
BAKELITE, 6 TUBES, 2 BANDS
BROWN OR PAINTED $30

ZENITH 313 CA1939
'BULLET'
BAKELITE, 4 TUBES, 1 BAND, DC
BROWN $100, BLACK $125

ZENITH 314 CA1939
'BULLET'
BAKELITE, 4 TUBES, 1 BAND, DC
BROWN $125, BLACK $150

ZENITH 311 CA1939
'TURRET'
BAKELITE, 4 TUBES, 1 BAND, DC
BROWN OR PAINTED $125
BLACK $150

ZENITH 312 CA1939
'TURRET'
BAKELITE, 5-6 TUBES, 1 BAND
BROWN OR PAINTED $225
BLACK $250

ZENITH 516 CA1941
BAKELITE, 6 TUBES, 2 BANDS
BROWN OR PAINTED $125

ZENITH 511 CA1941
BAKELITE, 6 TUBES, 2 BANDS
BROWN OR PAINTED $40

ZENITH 413,414 CA1940
'UPSIDE-DOWN CHASSIS'
PAINTED BAKELITE, 6 TUBES, 1 BAND
BROWN $225, MAHOGANY $250
GRAY $250, GREEN $275

ZENITH 411,416 CA1940
'UPSIDE-DOWN CHASSIS'
PAINTED BAKELITE, 6 TUBES, 1 BAND
BROWN $175, MAHOGANY $200
GRAY $200, GREEN $225

ZENITH 520,610 CA1941
BAKELITE, 5 TUBES, 1 BAND
BROWN OR PAINTED $40

ZENITH 611 CA1942
BAKELITE, 5 TUBES, 1 BAND
BROWN OR PAINTED $40

ZENITH 612,631 CA1942
BAKELITE, 5 TUBES, 1 BAND
BROWN OR PAINTED $40

ZENITH 614 CA1942
BAKELITE, 5 TUBES, 1 BAND
BROWN OR PAINTED $50

ZENITH 616 CA1942
BAKELITE, 5 TUBES, 1 BAND
BROWN OR PAINTED $75

ZENITH 617 CA1942
4 TUBES, 1 BAND, DC
BROWN OR PAINTED $40

ZENITH 918 CA1950
BAKELITE, 5 TUBES, 1 BAND
BROWN OR PAINTED $30

ZENITH 920 CA1950
BAKELITE, 8 TUBES, AM-FM
BROWN $25

ZENITH 921,922 CA1950
BAKELITE, 8 TUBES, AM-FM
BROWN $20

**ZENITH A402 CA1958
'SEASHORE'**
STYRENE, 5 TUBES, 1 BAND
BLACK $20, TAN $25, PINK $50

**ZENITH A501, B510 CA1959
'LANCER'**
STYRENE, 5 TUBES, 1 BAND
BLACK $20, IVORY $20, GREEN $40

ZENITH A515 CA1958
PAINTED BAKELITE, 5 TUBES, 1 BAND,
TAN $25, BLACK $30, GREEN $50, WHITE $30,
BLACK+RED $75

**ZENITH A516 CA1959
'DELUXE'**
STYRENE, 5 TUBES, 1 BAND,
WHITE $20, TAN $20, GRAY $25

**ZENITH B508 CA1959
'MAJORETTE'**
STYRENE, 5 TUBES, 1 BAND
WHITE $15, MAROON $25

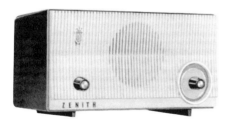

**ZENITH B509 CA1959
'ASCOT'**
STYRENE, 5 TUBES, 1 BAND
GREEN $30, YELLOW $40, RED $60, GRAY $20

**ZENITH B511 CA1959
'TRUMPETEER'**
STYRENE, 5 TUBES, 1 BAND
TAN $20, AQUA $50, YELLOW $65, ORANGE $75

ZENITH B513 CA1959
'TOREODOR'
STYRENE, 5 TUBES, 1 BAND
IVORY $20, BLACK $25
GREEN $35, ORANGE $50

ZENITH B514,515 CA1959
STYRENE, 5 TUBES, 1 BAND,
BLACK $40, WHITE $40
GRAY $40, PINK $60, BLUE $70
YELLOW $80, GREEN $60

ZENITH B615 CA1957
'COTILLION'
STYRENE, 5 TUBES, 1 BAND
YELLOW $45, GREEN $30, GRAY $20

ZENITH C519 CA1959
'NOCTURNE'
STYRENE, 5 TUBES, 1 BAND,
BLACK $25, TAN $25, YELLOW $50, WHITE $20

ZENITH G510 CA1950
BAKELITE, 5 TUBES, 1 BAND
BROWN $30

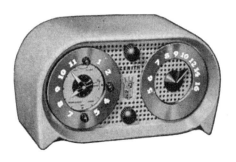

ZENITH G516 CA1950
5 TUBES, 1 BAND
BROWN BAKELITE $50
IVORY PLASKON $75

ZENITH G516 CA1950
BAKELITE, 5 TUBES, 1 BAND
BROWN OR PAINTED $25

ZENITH G725 CA1950
BAKELITE, 8 TUBES, AM-FM
BROWN OR PAINTED $25

ZENITH H511 CA1951
'RACE TRACK'
BAKELITE, 5 TUBES, 1 BAND
BROWN OR PAINTED $50

ZENITH H511V CA1955
'CARNIVAL'
STYRENE, 5 TUBES, 1 BAND
IVORY $30, BLACK $40, TAN $35, RED $100

ZENITH H516 CA1950
BAKELITE, 5 TUBES, 1 BAND
BROWN OR PAINTED $30

ZENITH H723 CA1950
BAKELITE, 8 TUBES, AM-FM
BROWN OR PAINTED $20

ZENITH J616,K515,K518,Y514 CA1952
PAINTED BAKELITE, 5-6 TUBES, 1 BAND,
BROWN $35, BLACK $45
IVORY $40, BLUE $60

**ZENITH K412R CA1953
'CREST'**
4 TUBES, 1 BAND, DC
PAINTED BAKELITE+METAL GRILLE
BROWN $150, BLACK $175
IVORY $150, MAROON $175

ZENITH K622 CA1953
PAINTED BAKELITE, 6 TUBES, 1 BAND
BROWN $30, BLACK $40
IVORY $40

**ZENITH M403 CA1952
'ZENETTE'**
PAINTED BAKELITE+METAL GRILLE
4 TUBES, 1 BAND, DC
BROWN $50, BLACK $60
IVORY $60, MAROON $70

ZENITH ROYAL 850 CA1957
STYRENE, TRANSISTOR, 1 BAND, DC,
BLACK $30, IVORY $35
TAN $35, PINK $60

ZENITH X509V CA1956
STYRENE, 5 TUBES, 1 BAND
IVORY $45, BLACK $50, GRAY $45
GREEN $60, RED $100

ZENITH Y519 CA1956
STYRENE, 5 TUBES, 1 BAND
IVORY $30, BLACK $40, GRAY $35
PINK $60, RED $90

**ZENITH Z615F CA1958
'ZEPHYR'**
STYRENE, 5 TUBES, 1 BAND
WHITE $35, GRAY $40, GREEN $60

ZENITH 'ZENETTE' CA1953
STYRENE+METAL TRIM, 4 TUBES, 1 BAND, DC
BROWN $60, BLACK $70
MAROON $85

ZENITH F508A CA1960
STYRENE, 5 TUBES, 1 BAND
BLACK $15, IVORY $15, GRAY $20
PINK $40, CORAL $45

ZEPHYR 35X5 CA1938
5 TUBES, 2 BANDS
BLACK BAKELITE $250
IVORY PLASKON $350

ZEPHYR 1 CA1960
STYRENE, 4 TUBES, 1 BAND
WHITE $20, BLACK $30
PINK $45, AQUA $55